A HOME FOR MIN SOO

A Home for Min Soo

Putting Together the Pieces of My Life

KIM, MIN SOO

With
Brian and Sarah Hampshire

The Fourth One Publishing

Paperback ISBN: 979-8-9884345-0-4
eBook ISBN: 979-8-9884345-1-1
Audiobook ISBN: 979-8-9884345-3-5

Cover Design: Hannah Linder Designs

Foreword: Trisha White Priebe, Author

First Printing, 2023

CONTENTS

CONCLUSION

DEDICATION

Mrs. Choi, "Omma," mother of my heart—and her family
My birth parents for giving me life
Dad, Mom, my siblings, and nieces & nephews for being a loving family

IN MEMORY

"Mrs. Martha" for giving time, skills, & care
Grandma for being so loving

"Sometimes you just have to be at a place
because God wants you there. It's your purpose."
—Benjamin D. Hampshire
a.k.a. Kim, Min Soo

Foreword

Dear reader, you hold in your hands a book written by a young man with whom I share something profoundly personal—Min and I were both adopted. We were born to unwed mothers in extraordinarily difficult circumstances but were given the privilege *to live*.

And we're so very grateful for this.

As you'll read in these precious pages, Min's path hasn't been an easy one.

Not even close.

Though deeply loved and cherished by his family and those privileged enough to call him *friend*, Min has faced more hurdles in thirty years than many face in a lifetime. And it's quite possible his greatest challenges still lie ahead.

So, when Min says he's glad he's adopted and truly happy with the life he's living, *that should mean something.*

I was first introduced to Min in 2011 when my husband and I were adopting our oldest son from Thailand. In 2014, Min graciously sent us a gift the same week he had a medical port implanted for chemotherapy. *This sums up Min in a single example.*

He's endlessly funny, curious, and generous.

Writing is hard work, even for those of us who love collecting words and phrases and arranging them on the page. Min did the excruciating work—exploring nooks and crannies of his past, sitting with his thoughts, quieting his doubts, telling his story, forgiving those who hurt him long ago, and *telling the truth.*

Min's story *should absolutely* be told.

Once I held *A Home for Min Soo*, I couldn't put it down. I'm convinced you'll love it—*and love Min*—as I do.

Warning: If you read this book, you run the risk of being changed for the better.

—Trisha White Priebe*

*Author of numerous books and co-author with Jerry B. Jenkins, Communication Coordinator for *Lifesong for Orphans*, and Blogger at RightWhereYouBelong.com

Note from Min's Scribes

When Min Soo expressed wanting to write his story, he did so with great resolve.

The first few times we sat to record his thoughts were "interesting," to say the least. The "secretary" persuaded him to relinquish control of the computer keyboard and to dictate instead.

Min Soo repeated some words so often, those alone could fill a book. Thus, we opted to remove most repeats and shortened run-on sentences (with his permission). Other alterations clarified timing or meaning. We didn't wish to damage his "voice," so pronouns and verbs remain as he uses them.

Min Soo loves using large words but doesn't always understand them. We became the "vocabulary police," enforcing this rule: "You can only use a word if you know its definition." There were times, though, the "police" turned their heads and let the "felon" have his way—some words too good to ignore!

We used visual aids to engage Min Soo. A small globe with three sticky-note arrows—one for God placed on top, one for Min Soo on South Korea, and one for his adoptive family on the United States—helped him realize God orchestrated east meeting west. He couldn't resist laughing, though, as he moved those willy-nilly around the world.

Another tool? A jigsaw puzzle. Min Soo removed a piece for each chapter completed to see his progress.

We used umpteen scratch pads, drawing timelines and illustrations, to aid Min Soo in grasping certain situations. And true to form, he kept multiple pencils nearby.

Min Soo wanted quotes in his book "like a real author." He and his "hired help" collected many from which Min Soo carefully chose. Min read these to the "secretary," which became more challenging as seizure medication kicked in and his speech slurred.

At the start of this venture, Min Soo brought stress toys to the table. After day one, the Rubik's cube lay in pieces—a warning of things to come! The stress ball followed suit, ending its career. And stuffed "little kitty" lost inches off her waist.

Min Soo also "took field trips" to recapture emotions of certain events in his life. To understand himself as a toddler, he observed a boy that age. Next, Min Soo interviewed a birth mother to sense what his own likely felt.

Interspersed with Min Soo's story are letters in italics, relaying background and insights into his lows and highs, sorrows and joys, challenges and victories.

While working with Min Soo, we discovered much more about him and marveled at how he accomplished this writing challenge. We thank him for bringing us along and now introduce you to this exceptional young man.

Sincerely,
Brian and Sarah Hampshire

Note from the Author

I'm a child in a man's body. My thirty-year-old self lives with developmental disability and more. I'm also a mix of life and death. My life is a time bomb. I won't reach old man age, so I went to my parents and said, "I want to write my story. I think God let me live this long because it's part of my purpose."

My journey went through dire circumstances, but I know God has a purpose for everything that happened in my life. I hope my story is a testimony to you about how God takes this journey with me.

Sincerely,

Kim, Min Soo

How to Pronounce Korean Words in This Book:

Kim, Min Soo = "GKim" between hard "G" & soft "K," "Meen Sooh" like "oo" in "book"

Cho = close like "(Ch)Joe" sounds ("Ch" is almost silent)

Pusan = "Poo-sahn"& Seoul = "Soe-uhl"

Choi, Jung Hee = "Chwei, Yung Hee" & Omma = "oh-mah" (mommy)

kimchi = "kim-chee" (a Korean food)

Appa = "ahp-bah" (daddy)

Yun Kuk-Yong = "Yoon Kook-Yong" ani = "ah-nee" (no)

Halmoni = "Hae(l)-muh-nee," almost silent "L" (Grandma) gamsa-hapnida = "gahm-sah-ham-nee-dah" (thank you)

Taeguk = "Tay-gooh" (sports team name)

Kkeut = "Goo(t)" –Strong "G"-sound, "oo" as in book, & soft "T" (The End)

Seon Joo So = "Sun-Joe-So"

| 1 |

How I Became Me

"To be loved and to be cared for ... to be wanted
... this is the heart of every orphan."
—*Steve Morrison* (Korean adoptee)[1]

I am number 93-89 SHK. That's because I was born in 1993 and was the eighty-ninth baby that year put up for adoption by the Social Welfare Society.[a] I feel like I was made from a machine because of so many babies being born and adopted. They sent babies all around the world—but not baby 93-89.

I was born with a problem. Brown spots. The doctors wondered why I had them, so they sent me to another hospital where they tried to figure out what was wrong. They shaved the top of my head, like the other babies there, because that's what they did. We all looked like little old men—even the girls.

Because of all this, I would have a hard time finding family. My head size was bigger than the other babies. That made things even worse for me. I was at that hospital about one month.

I don't remember anything about being born because babies don't remember that. I know pieces of information because some of my history came with me each place I went.

Why did Korea not let my birth mother keep me? She was my biological mother. I don't have a grudge against her. She did what was best for me. She loved me well enough, but it all didn't seem fair.

Her name was Kim, ___ ___. In Korea, the last name is always first. She lived about sixty miles from Pusan (now Busan). That's where she met my birth father. His name was Cho, ___ ___. My birth parents were both at age twenty-five when I was born. I don't understand why my birth father left unborn-me and my birth mother, but he did. I feel sad about it because he split.

My birth parents weren't married. When I was old enough and curious, I asked how I became me. At first, I asked only small questions that matched my size. Later I asked bigger ones because I grew bigger too.

When I found out what my birth parents "did," I was enraged to the point I wanted nothing to do with them. I felt like I was a sin. What was going through their minds when they had sex and created me, making me feel like a bad word!

Why couldn't my birth mother be accepted into South Korea's society because she was pregnant? I don't understand that, but she went to the birth mothers' home (that's what they call the unwed mothers' place) where workers helped her and other pregnant ladies and, in some of these, continued teaching them after babies were born.[2]

Then came time for me to be born.

I, Kim Min Soo, was born on Tuesday, March 9th, 1993 in Pusan. If my birth father stayed, my name would be Cho and I would have been recognized as a citizen, not illegitimate. But he didn't.

So, my birth mother had no choice but to send me up for adoption. Here I am coming out as a baby, which I'm a person, and my country wouldn't let me be a citizen because my father walked out on me. I was born and I am nothing. All I wanted was a blanket, milk, and love. I didn't belong.

When it was time for my birth mother to leave me, it must have hurt her deeply. During my growing-up years, I wondered why my birth mother did this. Did she cry when she gave me away? To this day

I wonder if she still thinks about me wherever she is. On my birthday is she sad?

I left the place of my birth. My case worker or an escort took me to the train station where we boarded and went to Seoul. It was a very long ride. Maybe I cried along the way. Maybe the motion and sounds comforted me. I don't know, but we got there.

Precious Min Soo,

I have loved you with an everlasting love. You are so special to Me. I care for the tiniest sparrow that falls from a tree, yet I care oh so much more for tiny you.

When you began growing in your mother's womb, I already knew all about you. I knitted you together in that dark place. Before you were born, I knew what every single day of your life would hold. I had a plan for you—a future, a Hope. I still do.

Now you are leaving everything you've known and not known. Your mother. Your absent father. Yet be assured, Min Soo. When your father forsook you, you still had a Father. I AM your Abba. When your mother surrendered you, I wrapped My Arms around you like a mother bird, sheltering her young. I hold you still and send angels to guard you.

I know you full well—from how many hairs are on your head to each thought you will think—also each step taken, each hurt endured, each joy celebrated. I AM with you always. You will never walk alone.

I AM your God. I AM and will become your salvation. Rest in these promises. Where you are, I AM also. Now, precious infant, we're on our way to a place I've designed just for you.

With all My love,
Your Heavenly Father [b]

FYI:

[a] SWS—Min's Korean-side adoption agency

(b) From Jeremiah 31:3, Matthew 6:26, Psalm 139:2-6, 13-16, Jeremiah 29:11, Psalm 27:10, Galatians 4:6, Psalm 63:7, Psalm 34:7, Luke 12:7, Hebrews 13:5, Matthew 28:20, Isaiah 44:6, Isaiah 12:2, Acts 17:28, Psalm 23:1-6

| 2 |

A Bundle of Joy and Other Things

"He is an orphan and needs a good home ..." (Betty Rubble)
—from The Flintstones [3]

In Seoul, I was assigned to a foster mother who took forty-day-old me, hoping I would be adopted soon. Her name was Mrs. Choi—wife and mother in the Hong family.[c] Mrs. Choi was a Christian who loved God. She had two teen sons and a husband who worked at a job. She took care of many babies before me.

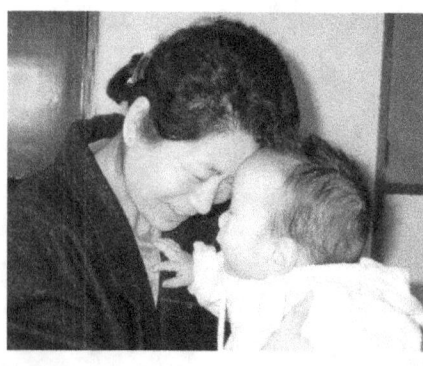

Mrs. Choi wrapped me to herself and carried me about, like all Korean mothers do—mostly on her back. I liked that best. She dressed me in nice clothes, and I ate a lot and gained good weight—good news for my monthly check-ups at the SWS hospital. But there were still problems—my brown spots and head size. I also wasn't doing things as fast as other babies.

I took a liking to Mrs. Choi and her family. They liked me too. They felt I was their family, and I didn't know any different.

Then my time came to be adopted! A lady from United States wanted me to be her son. She filled out paperwork for SWS. Mrs. Choi was pleased because getting me adopted was the goal. By now I was there a half year.

Things seemed to go well. Then boom! The lady didn't want me anymore.

This was bad but good too. I wouldn't get adopted right now, but I would stay with Mrs. Choi in the Hong household. They were family I could cling to because they loved me very much. This was a wonderful deal!

As I grew, my foster mother took me to many checkups. During one appointment, doctors became more concerned. My brown spots weren't going away, I had freckling in areas I don't want to talk about and under my arms, my head was growing, and scans showed "cold spots" [d] on my kidneys.

HAPPY BIRTHDAY TO ME! I was still waiting for family. Months went by and nothing, but I was happy with my foster mother and her family because I thought they were mine and that this was my home. Mrs. Choi loved having me in her household; but she knew the longer I stayed, the harder it would be for me to find family.

Mrs. Choi worried because she cared for me like a son, and she became "mother" to me. As I formed words, I called her "Omma," Korean for "mommy."

Omma took me to the grocery store. She bought my favorite foods—kimchi, fish, rice, fruits, and soda—anything I wanted. I shook my hands in the air and grabbed foods, but Omma didn't scold me. She spoiled me rotten, like a little king.

I lived in an apartment building. When I became a good walker, Omma let me visit neighbors in other apartments. She took me to the playground with another boy. We played together.

I often bumped my forehead because I climbed on things I shouldn't and fell. I was like the Tasmanian Devil,[4] always running around. Omma struggled to keep up with me but loved me no matter what.

HAPPY BIRTHDAY TO ME! I turned two years old.

When I wasn't playing and getting into mischief, I went to many medical appointments.

At Seoul National University Hospital, they discovered a problem in my brain. They did tests on me because it looked like I might have neurofibromatosis type 1 (NF1) due to my genetics. Omma didn't understand because she thought I was "so clever and smart."

Now they knew this was more complicated. This genetic disease had something to do with nerves and tumors. (A person with NF1 can grow tumors on any nerve in their body.)

In Spring 1995, the SWS case worker called Omma and told her to "prepare for certain change." They would be sending me to a "baby's reception home"—an orphanage "for hard cases." I was two-years-old and a little more, so I didn't understand, but Omma's voice was different when she told them, "I raised Min Soo for adoption, not placement to an orphanage at all." [5]

After the other family members came home, Omma shared about the phone call. They were sad and discouraged because they would lose me who was like their own kin.

From that moment Omma had trouble sleeping. Then she said to herself, "Stop worrying, stop weeping ... start to pray (to) God." [e] She poured her heart out to God alone at every dawn and at mealtimes with me.

"Dear Heavenly Father Who knows Min Soo so well, help us find loving, nice Christian adoptive parents so Min Soo will not be sent to orphanage." (f)

In the same spring on the other side of the world this was happening—

A family tells their story:

We received the Spring 1995 newsletter from "Neurofibroma-tosis Ink." [6] We had a couple children suspected of having a genetic "cousin" to neurofibromatosis—NF—so we subscribed to several agencies' publications to educate us.

This particular issue caught my eye. On front—a small article, titled "A Home for Min Soo," read:

"A loving family is needed to adopt a special little boy, Min Soo, who is waiting in Korea ... He is best described as 'Mr. Personality.' Min Soo is strongly suspected of having neuro-fibromatosis which classifies him as a special needs child."

The article explained adoption fees for special needs children were negotiable. Americans for International Aid and Adoption [g] (AIAA) gave their contact information.

I mentioned this ad to my husband and then laid it aside. From time to time, I read it again.

Summer 1995—South Korea

Omma continues to pray four times each day. SWS files adoption and immigration papers with AIAA in United States.

Summer 1995—United States

Curiosity got the best of me. I called the agency and left a message on their answering machine, saying I wondered if this little boy was adopted, gave our phone number, and hung up.

My husband and I packed to go in two different directions, he speaking at one children's Bible camp and I at another. We'd arrive home on different days, he returning first. As we scurried about, I commented, "Oh, by the way, if we get a call from an adoption agency, don't worry."

My husband stopped dead in his tracks. "If we what?"

I often threw out ideas, making him wonder what he committed to seventeen years earlier. "I just wanted to see if that little boy got adopted."

"He'll be hard to place. Who's going to adopt a kid with NF?" he questioned.

"We would?"

Brian and I had years of experience with special needs children. We understood a lot about NF—specialists it required, educational challenges it might present, life issues that could develop. NF didn't scare us.

What did scare me was Min Soo's age—two! We joked about having a toddler "at our age" then headed separate ways for the next two weeks.

Upon arriving home, I found a note from Brian. "Agency called. Little boy still available. Surprised?" Brian phoned that evening. We agreed to pray and talk about this when we settled home again.

We no longer owned small children's things—just an old wooden highchair in the attic—and lacked money for an adoption, even with special needs "discounts." As missionaries, our total source of income came from donating churches and individuals—often barely meeting our needs.

One night, during our praying week, I dreamt about David and Mephibosheth. This stirred me awake. I opened my Bible and read the account in II Samuel 9—King David searching for an heir to his like-a-brother friend, Jonathan. He found one—Mephibosheth, Jonathan's disabled son—and took him in as family, restoring Mephibosheth's rightful position in the royal household.

And there it was! David invited Mephibosheth to sit at his table all the days of his life.

We had a highchair. "Lord, are You saying all we need to do is invite Min Soo to sit at our table?"

His Word assured us we lacked nothing.

A few days later Brian returned. He wasn't home long when he asked, "So what should we do about that little boy? He needs a home. How 'bout ours?"

"I've been thinking a lot about it—but a two-year-old?"

"Two-year-olds grow up." Then Brian told me about his week and also his thoughts concerning this child. "What do we have left for a toddler?"

"A highchair. That's all."

"And enough love," he added.

We prayed, if this wasn't God's Will, He Alone would close doors. Door One opened when our four children agreed to add a brother—the start of many doors opening. We invited Min Soo to "sit at our table."

Autumn 1995—South Korea

Omma went to America for three weeks to learn more about AIAA adoptions. I stayed with a neighbor, but I wondered where Omma was. I was anguished.

When Omma returned, I ran and clung to her with my life. For weeks, I didn't want Omma out of my sight. If she was, I wailed.

The next month I went into the hospital because my head was growing too much. I might need surgery. What a nightmare! Here I am, and Omma isn't with me again! I was distraught.

Then SWS stopped any hope of adoption for me. I don't know why, but doctors told Omma devastating news. She pleaded with them to do everything possible to help me.

Omma's heart is torn apart. Her most desire for me to find family is broken into pieces.

Autumn 1995—United States

AIAA assigns us a case worker. Paperwork and home study underway. Then we're notified Korea halted this adoption due to Min Soo possibly needing a shunt and suspicion of another genetic disease—this one fatal with deteriorating physical and mental ability—death at a young age.

Even though we aren't officially Min Soo's family, we weep over this little one who already feels like a son. After more prayer, we tell our case worker we still want to adopt Min Soo, even if he's going to die.

Winter 1995-1996—South Korea

I was happy eating my favorite foods, playing in the snow, and being spoiled by Omma. She still showed me great love and prayed alone at dawn and at meals with me. She was a tough lady full of faith and didn't give up. She begged SWS to let me stay longer even though my foster care was expiring.[h]

HAPPY BIRTHDAY TO ME! I'm three-years-old. Omma made me a cake. She looked happy on the outside, but inside she was saddened. Her time with me would soon end. That's how foster care was in South Korea. I would go to the orphanage "for hard cases."

March 14th, 1996

Omma prayed at dawn. She said, "In the morning, I was given a call by SWS, and it was a piece of happy news that Min Soo was matched with his adoptive parents. Then, we should be happy and laugh, but we were all crying with such good news." [i] Omma's prayers were answered!

Winter 1995-1996—United States

More meetings with our case worker and setting up a room for Min Soo! He'll bunk with hopeful brother Stephen.

SWS expresses concern about parents in their forties, but the process continues. God works amazingly, providing adoption fees and doing miracles on both sides of the world.

Spring 1996—South Korea

When I was an infant until I was almost three, SWS made short videos of me. They sent them to United States. My adoptive parents will see they're getting a doozy!

SWS wants my new family to send a book about them with pictures. Because I'm older, it might help me get to know them a little before I depart from South Korea.

Spring 1996—United States

AIAA tells us to get Mongolian spots [j] documented when Min Soo arrives—small one on his wrist and large one across his upper buttocks.

We make the requested family book for Min Soo and mail it.

While we await our three-year-old, several friends donate little boys' clothing, a car seat, and trike.

We view videos of Min Soo and note he indeed is "Mr. Personality!" Yet we're alarmed by the clip showing his distress when Mrs. Choi returns from the States.

We ask God to provide for one of us to travel to Min Soo rather than an escort bringing him.

God answers. Brian will do "labor and delivery" this time!

FYI:

[c] In Korea married women keep their maiden names and only change their title to Mrs.

[d] NY doctors couldn't interpret this, even after seeing Min's Korean scans.

[e] Direct quote from Mrs. Choi, Jung Hee

[f] Direct quote from Mrs. Choi, Jung Hee

[g] AIAA—Min's American-side adoption agency

[h] South Korean foster care expires at age three. If unadopted by then, a child is placed in an orphanage.

[i] Direct quote from Mrs. Choi, Jung Hee

[j] Common birthmark with Asian children, resembling a bruise but disappearing over time

| 3 |

My Whole New World

"The Milky Way and a small, white boat ...
In the blue Sky—Without a sail or an oar—
... sails through the sky swiftly—Toward the western land."
—Yun Kuk-Yong [7]

A special book arrived, and Omma sat me on her lap. The first page is a circle with stick-figure-me in Korea and stick-family on the other side. Omma said, even though I didn't understand, there's family waiting for me in United States, and she moves her finger from stick-me across to stick-family. Omma told me the blue color is water, which I know now the circle was the world.

Omma pointed to the tall stick-man, which she called "Appa," and to the stick-lady and said she was "Mama," then one-two-three brothers and a sister. She then pointed at a house and explained I will live there. Three-year-old me didn't understand because I lived with Omma.

She started packing my stuff and cried at the same time, and I didn't know why. She gave me all my favorite foods, and she prayed but it was different now—a mix of sad and happy. Her words were different too. She prayed I would "adjust to new environment and forget

Korea."[k] She was happy I will be adopted but, at the same time, sad I must leave her.

A tall man arrived and a Korean lady I saw at SWS. Omma followed me around, cleaning up my soda mess because I spilled my can of cola everywhere—on me too—as she tried changing my clothes. They came in, and Omma says the tall man is Appa like in the book.

The next time I saw Appa was at the SWS building on the seventh floor very high up. I tried to climb out the window, but Appa grabbed me and put me on his lap. I was so wiggly and climbed off, and Omma gave me treats to keep me in one place.

Me and Omma had a mother-son relationship. She treated me like her own, and I saw her as my mother since I had no remembering of my birth mother. I was with Omma three years, probably the longest any baby stayed with her.

Omma's prayers were answered. I found a family. Then Omma grieved because she might never see me again. I was her foster child, but to her I was a son of her heart.

Now two mothers lost a son. My birth mother lost her own flesh and blood because that's what I was. Omma, on the other hand, lost the son of her heart due to caring for me such a long time. That grieved them deeply and still might to this day.

South Korea—May 18th, 1996

Omma bought me new clothes to fly to America—an American flag shirt, jeans shorts, and brand-new shoes. I looked so cute!

Appa and me rode in a taxi to the airport. I saw lots of people and heard lots of noises. Outside big windows were huge planes. I pointed at each one and said, "Ping-gae!" [l] I knew that because Omma showed me what ping-gae was and told me I was going in one. I used to see planes flying over the apartments when we played outside.

I will ride in ping-gae then go home to Omma. Appa carried me in one arm and a suitcase in the other. I wore my backpack with a change of clothes and favorite snacks and carried my small, green, cloth bag full of little toy cars. Time to get on the plane! My three-year-old self was excited. My eyes went everywhere!

Soon we flew high in the sky, and I saw the world below. It was even more exciting than riding my trike! The plane went up-up-up until we were in the clouds. I was super happy!

The plane kept moving-moving-moving. The longer we were in the sky, more time passed, and I fell asleep.

When I woke up, I became frantic and uncontrollable. *Enough ping-gae! I want to go home.* But the plane kept going to its destination. *Where's Omma? Why doesn't ping-gae take me to her? This isn't fun anymore.* I cried in deep distress—like I lost something. *Maybe Omma is coming to take me home.* But she didn't arrive. I was terrified!

Omma tried to explain to me (with the special book) that I will live with new family far away, but I didn't understand—not really. I was totally clueless except that something was missing. Omma.

A lady like Omma held me. She spoke softly in my native tongue and calmed me. The hum of the ping-gae and her soothing me with my head on her chest, rubbing my back, felt like being with Omma—and I fell asleep again.

Dear Delta Flight Attendants,   *May 18th, 1996*

My three-year-old whirlwind swept through the airport waiting area—showing everyone his little green cloth bag filled with Matchbox cars. When we boarded the plane, you really earned your pay!

I carried Min Soo. You led us to our seats and gave him cookies—one of many treats you brought. I managed to get seat belts around us both with your help.

Then out came the cars! I apologize for the runaway vehicles as Min Soo enjoyed dumping them repeatedly—all of you scrambling to retrieve them as they careened down the aisle.

Afterwhile, we settled into a routine, including multiple trips to the bathroom on this 5,265-mile flight. Then Min Soo ran his favorite car up and down the seat, the floor, and his new dad.

As passengers quieted for the night, you handed us blankets and pillows then caught your breath as I rocked my boy to sleep.

After some time passed, Min Soo awoke, frantically pushed me away, and cried. Here we were—new dad with a tot who didn't speak English, taken away from everything he knew! It hit him with a vengeance!

My heart broke as I tried everything to comfort him to no avail. I wept for my little boy.

Across the aisle sat a Korean mother with a toddler. Her heart went out to us, and she opened her arms to comfort Min Soo.

After a while, she handed my sleeping son to me where he stayed until daylight. I was grateful for her kindness to a stranger. You thanked her and extended extra care to her as well.

You helped us deplane ahead of first class. Smiles were in abundance— of relief, no doubt. Thank you for every kindness. You treated us royally.

Sincerely,

Brian Hampshire—grateful parent

May 18th—Saturday. Ping-gae landed in Portland, Oregon, USA. Then another to New York City and one more to where I would live with Appa, Mama, and my new siblings.

Dear American Airline Attendants,   *May 19th, 1996*

Thank you for holding the plane since our connecting flight was canceled! Min delighted with the speed of our trek to the far end of the terminal. I was exhausted, struggling to carry this precious "cargo," but we made it!

From Portland to New York City, you were patient as my little imp dumped his bag of cars, laughing as they raced down the aisle. I'm sure you were glad the flight wasn't longer.

You came to hear our story when you learned I was bringing this little one home to become family.

Our flight from New York City to Syracuse was a puddle-jumper. I sat with my head tilted to keep from hitting the ceiling. Min Soo was restless, his bag of cars no longer entertaining him. Thankfully, it was a short flight.

As we landed, severe wind and heavy rain hit. The plane skidded sideways down the runway. I prayed, "God, help. I didn't come halfway around the earth to die with Min Soo so near home!" God delivered the plane safely.

Thank you for getting us home—my son for the very first time. You were wonderful with him.

Sincerely,

Brian Hampshire—weary, frazzled parent

1:00 a.m. Sunday, May 19th, 1996: Time to get off the ping-gae. Appa picked me up and carried me through the tube hallway to where a big girl and new omma waited. I wasn't sure about them. I was afraid and grabbed Appa.

Appa said, "Min Soo," and pointed to the new omma, "this is Mama."

Mama reached her arms out, and I went to her. Mama said, "Welcome to America."

"Amicka." I looked back at Appa with worried eyes and reached for him.

Mama let me go, and Appa carried me to get our luggage. The big girl came too. She was from the special book Omma used to teach me about my new family.

When we arrived at the van, Appa strapped me in a car seat. Then he got in the driver's seat and flipped on low lights inside. Those calmed me. The big girl sat nearby and handed me little toys. I was still scared, but at least Appa was there. I was quiet the rest of the trip to my new home.

We pulled in the driveway, and Appa came to me and said, "Min Soo, we're home." I didn't know what he was saying. Appa carried me up to the house, we all went inside, and he set me down.

There were two sleepy big same-boys (m) waiting—from the special book. Another boy came downstairs rubbing his eyes. He was in the book too.

Then this furry thing pranced toward me, wagging its tail. I kicked it. The furry thing backed off. I sat down, pulled off my brand-new shoes, and placed them at the door like Omma taught me.

I jumped up and ran full throttle throughout the house. Rooms connected to each other. I ran from dining room to living room to kitchen, dining room, living room, kitchen—repeat!

My siblings were flabbergasted at this munchkin running crazy, laughing evilly, and yelling. Mama sat there shaking her head. I didn't have any clue what she said, but later she told me, "What have we gotten ourselves into!"

I kept running-running-running until I ran out of energy.

Then Appa got me ready for bed. Mama took me by the hand and showed me to a little mat on the floor by Appa's side of the bed. I ran out of the room, grabbed my little green bag of cars, and laid back on the mat. Then I curled up into the fetal position and moaned like I lost something dear to me. My bag of cars became my link to Korea and my substitute Omma.

Mama laid next to me on the bed rubbing my back. I pushed her hand away. Then she patted my back, and I pushed her away again. Next, she put a blanket on me. I kicked it off. She hummed songs, and I fell asleep.

It was light outside when I woke up and went to Appa. He cleaned me up and got me dressed. Then he took me to the kitchen and put me on a high-up wooden chair. I sat cross-legged because of my Korean culture. Appa then prayed. I didn't understand what he said, but I knew "pray" because Omma prayed with me at every meal.

Mama gave me snacks from Omma as well as food she bought at the Korean market. When I saw the food, I shouted, "choo-sayo,"[n] which means "please give me." I wanted second breakfast, and I said "choo-sayo" again, and Mama used sign language. She put her fingers straight and made them like closed claws, tapping the ends of her fingers against one another, and said "more." I caught on immediately and tried to sign.

This is how I started learning English. My family showed me sign language and said the word. They taught me "wait, stop, more, please, sorry, thank you, now, later, toilet."

Both my family and I had to understand what I was saying in Korean.

Omma wrote a long letter and explained what "shee" and "unga" meant because my new family needed to know bathroom terms. She told Appa I was potty-trained, but she sent some Pull-Ups with me to America. (Potty-trained kids who were just adopted could digress because of grieving. I was among them.)

I ran to the door and put my shoes on to go outside. Mama brought some toys out onto our big front cement stoop.

I kept saying "chimmy" [o] and pointed to peonies next to the stoop. So Mama thought, *Chimmy is flower.* Then I saw ants and spiders and said "chimmy," stomped on them, and laughed. Now Mama knew chimmy was bug. This was how my family started understanding my foreign language.

My family kept me busy during the day, but at night feelings rushed back. I laid on my bed mat, embraced my little bag full of cars, curled up with my bottom in the air, and moaned.

I still wasn't sure about Mama. *Omma will come for me.* Mama was on the bed next to me. She hummed but didn't rub my back because I didn't like it and pushed her away.

The fourth day, when I woke up, Appa washed and dressed me. Mama was in the kitchen cooking. I climbed up onto my high-up chair, crossed my legs, and ate breakfast.

Mama wiped tears. Appa comforted her and said something I didn't understand. Mama nodded, left the kitchen, and went out of the house.

New omma is crying.

Appa and me finished breakfast. Then he cleaned my face and hands, and I ran to the door and put on my shoes. I went outside onto the front stoop.

Mama was sitting on the edge with her feet on the stairs. I ran to her, sat down, and laid my head on her lap. Mama gently rubbed my back, and I let her. I stayed there a good chunk of time and felt like this was my mother.

I was right where I belonged.

Omma had prayed I would forget Korea and her family quickly. My new parents prayed I would adjust to them and all these changes. Both prayers were answered on Day Four.

To Canine-loving Humans: *Spring to Fall 1996*

I heard sounds and trip-tropped to the door. There stood a small human who gave me a swift kick. I backed away, and he let out a wicked laugh. He ran throughout the house, bonking me with a roll of wrapping paper! Then my master said strange words to him and took the roll away.

The small human disrupted everything. He ate my food and tossed it about. He took over my bed and left little toys on it. Sometimes he curled up and slept there like an innocent puppy.

One day, the small human grabbed doggy shampoo, rubbed it all over my head and back, and fled laughing. My master patted me, hesitated, and smelled his hand. Then he said the dreaded word "bath." Another time the small human used maple syrup! Yum! Maybe he wanted to help.

But sometimes the small human drove me bonkers! I gave him warnings. I didn't mean to make him cry. He complied after that, though, and now we're buddies. He doesn't throw my food anymore, but he still eats some.

While he's outside, I stay by him. When he comes in, I make sure he gets inside safely.

He sneaks me food at the table. Afterward, he tries to ride on me. That's where I draw the line. I still warn him, but I don't make him cry anymore. Before bed, he "reads" me a book about a dog that tries to be good. [8]

My nemesis, the cat, sleeps atop the recliner. My small human pushes the button on the side and launches the cat. This delights him no end, and me too!

—the clean, well-fed, amused family dog

FYI:

[k] Direct quote from Mrs. Choi, Jung Hee

[l] "Ping-gae"—how three-year-old Min pronounced airplane

[m] How Min perceived identical twin brothers, Nathan and Michael

[n] "Choo-sao"—how three-year-old Min pronounced please give me

[o] "Chimmy"—how three-year-old Min pronounced bug

| 4 |

"Ani-Ani!"

"Trouble ought to be my middle name."
—from "Hoomania" theme song[9]

In "Amicka" I had many doctors' appointments. Appa and Mama took me to a kids' doctor for a checkup and to have my Mongolian spots recorded, like AIAA told us to do.

Mama kept me busy with some toys and books. This doctor looked in my ears and mouth, listened to my heart, and checked my brown spots and Mongolian ones. Three-year-old me didn't understand because I still spoke full-on Korean, but this doctor was fun. I got a sticker and put it on my shirt.

Next came a special doctor called "neurologist"—Dr. Nancy. Two of my siblings knew her. She was kind. Peaceful-like.

Mama brought the same toys to this doctor's place. I only used these toys at special places so they stayed interesting. Dr. Nancy had a toy like one I played with at the SWS hospital in Korea. That made me happy.

Then she gave me a checkup—different from the other doctor. I sat on Appa's lap, and he held my head still. Dr. Nancy touched bright, hanging things and moved a light around to see if my eyes looked this way or that. She sat me on the exam table and bonked a little hammer-thing on me different places. I tried to grab it, so she let me bonk myself. I laughed.

Then she hit a silver metal thing (p) against her other hand. It hummed. She put it on the side of my head, and I freaked! It hummed weird the way I heard it inside myself. I pulled my head away and stared at that thing. I didn't like that one little bit!

She checked my brown spots, and my now self knows those were called café-au-lait spots or nicknamed "coffee spots." Mama and Appa like coffee.

Then Dr. Nancy looked under my arms. That tickled. She showed my parents tiny spots there and said that was another sign of neuro-fibromatosis type 1—NF1—and that they were likely in another area. Sure enough!

I didn't cooperate for her to check my spine. Appa stood up, bent over, and touched his toes, so I copied him. Then the doctor felt up and down my back, and I squirmed. It tickled, and I laughed. Dr. Nancy said we needed to keep an eye on that spine of mine, and my parents said they would take me to the chiropractor.

When it was over, the doctor said my NF1 diagnosis was for sure, but later I would need a brain scan. She said we would wait about six months until I became used to my new environment. Then Dr. Nancy made Appa and Mama super happy.

My now self understands my parents breathed relief-joy because the doctor told them, "There's no evidence of any fatal genetic disease." I was happy too because I could choose something from the prize box. I grabbed handfuls, but I could only take one. It was a hard choice.

Dr. Nancy told my parents I needed an eye checkup, so they took me. That was a challenge for me and the eye doctor too because I had to be still. We both survived. He discovered a little mark (q) on one eye—also proof of NF1.

After that, my parents needed a nap. Me too. I didn't mind because Mama signed, "First nap, then food." I didn't love nap, but I loved food, so I napped.

One more appointment—the chiropractor. He put me on a special table facing down and pushed on my spine. Then he flipped me over and moved my head this way and that with a jolt. My neck popped so loud, my parents heard it. I cried hard. Appa picked me up and comforted me.

Mama said, "Min, you made popcorn. Pop-pop-pop!" and did the sign for it. I stopped crying because I liked popcorn. From then on, I called the chiropractor "Dr. Popcorn," but I didn't much like it there.

I was just a munchkin and didn't understand. But my grown-up self has been through hundreds of checkups and scans. I was supposed to have the first scan after my next neurology appointment, but it didn't happen. Something else did that changed everything.

For now, I was just me, doing all the things a little kid does. Doing things I shouldn't either, but that's another story.

My first big trip in "Am-icka" was to meet Grandma at her eightieth birthday party. We drove a long way, and all Appa's side of the family came. Appa carried me over to Grandma. He gave her a hug.

Grandma gently put her hand on me and said words I didn't understand, except for "Min Soo." She spoke a soft way that I liked.

Appa placed his hand on Grandma's shoulder, looked at me, and said, "Halmoni. Grandma." He touched me and said, "Min Soo." Then he repeated it. I put the pieces together and pointed at her and said, "Hammoni. Gamma."

Halmoni was my only grandparent—a kind-hearted woman who would become an important figure in my life. She treated me equally to her other grandkids. I was real family to her.

My second trip in "Amicka" was very much longer than the first one. We went to meet Mama's side at a family reunion. I didn't have grandparents here, and Mama's sibling lived far, far away.

It was an outdoor picnic with many people and lots of food. There was a playground and room to run.

I loved the bouncy spring horses, tall slide but only the ladder part—I wouldn't slide down it—and merry-go-round. I sat right in the middle with my legs crossed and held onto the center pole. I laughed as I went around-around-around.

Appa and Mama were surprised I stayed in one spot so long. They never saw me do that. Everyone else asked, "Why isn't he getting sick?"

Afterwhile, Appa got his guitar to play music with a cousin. I ran to him. He moved the guitar, and I climbed onto his lap; then Appa put the guitar over us. I "helped" him play. Appa and the cousin sang.

At the family reunion, I could eat whatever I wanted. Chicken, noodles, and corn. Then I grabbed watermelon which I loved in South Korea with Omma.

Another big cousin was sitting in a child's wagon eating watermelon too. I ran over and sat with him. The big cousin took a bite and spit the seeds far.

I laid my pointer finger against my cheek, thought, and grinned. *This is my partner in crime. We get to spit food.* I spit seeds as far as I could and laughed maniacally.

The big cousin smiled. No one stopped us. I got away with this heinous act. Too good to be true!

The article my adoptive family saw about me needing a home said I was "Mr. Personality." Omma agreed and wrote in a letter, "Min Soo is famous for imp."

I no longer slept on the mat in my parents' room. Now I was upstairs on the bottom bunk with Stephen up top. My clothes and bed were upstairs, but my toys were downstairs.

When it was time to sleep, I wouldn't stay in my bed. Instead, I went in the upstairs bathroom, put random objects in the toilet, and laughed. Repeat-repeat-repeat! Each time my parents said, "Ani-ani!" which meant no-no. I was prohibited from going upstairs during the day because of causing mischief.

When I could go upstairs, Appa or Mama went too. They got me ready for bed. Then I laid on the floor next to them while we read a story and prayed. For a while, I fell asleep on the floor. My parent scooped me up and put me in bed. After a while, I climbed into bed on my own, but a parent stayed so I wouldn't wander.

In bed I listened to my parent hum songs. I reached down to whichever one took their turn that night and opened my hand. My parent held my hand in theirs, and I felt happy, like I belonged. Then I fell asleep.

One night I woke up, and there was a bit of light outside. I went downstairs, unlocked the front door, ran out, and headed down the street. I was so speedy and got four houses away. Our dog caught up to me. I was surprised because she was shut in the laundry room at night. Maybe she snuck out too.

Then I saw Mama coming. I ran to her laughing, and the dog followed.

Mama didn't look one little bit happy. She gave me a swift smack on my bottom and said sternly, "Ani-ani!"

I was alarmed! No one ever smacked me on the bottom because in South Korea I wasn't disciplined and got away with murder. I should've gotten the message not to do this again.

Appa went shopping and bought a chain lock. He put it on the door so I couldn't get out.

But next time I woke up in the night, went into the kitchen, grabbed my high-up chair, dragged it across the dining room to the front door, climbed up on it, and unhooked the chain. Appa had a hearing loss and didn't wake up, but Mama rushed out of the bedroom.

"Ani-ani!" She set me down and took the high-up chair into the kitchen.

Appa went shopping and bought an alarm. He installed it high on the door, out of my high-up chair reach. My escape plans were foiled until I discovered I could use the back door.

Appa went shopping and bought fencing. He closed in a play area for me. I was trapped.

Appa and Mama rested better after that.

One day Mama took me for a ride on a busy highway. I unbuckled my car seat, climbed down, and opened the van door. Mama quick as lightning pulled over. She came around, gave me a smack on the bottom, and buckled me into my car seat. Again "ani-ani!"

I didn't get many smacks on the bottom. Only when I put my life in danger because I wasn't afraid of anything. I was a dummkopf. Eventually I would learn, but it would take an extraordinarily long time.

Who thought I would try that again, but I did; so my parents added extra safety measures to my car seat. Foiled again!

I digressed with pottying. My parents rewarded me with M&Ms and gave me lots of praise for doing "shee" and "unga" where I should. But I was still mischievous—putting items in the toilet.

Mama bought Stephen and me little black toy phones with buttons that made music and sounds. I liked to push buttons.

One day I took Mama's hand and led her to the downstairs bathroom. She didn't have her glasses on. Mama saw a dark thing in the toilet, clapped, and said, "Very good boy!"

I was confused.

Mama flushed the toilet. The dark thing swirled around and started singing "London Bridge." Mama quick grabbed the dark thing because she now knew it wasn't "unga" because poop doesn't sing. Mama held the dripping toy over the toilet and yelled, "Brian!"

Appa came running!

I stood there, dumbfounded.

My parents tried not to laugh. Appa took the phone from Mama and went to toss it in the garbage, but Mama said, "Don't! I paid a whole dollar for that!"

Appa washed and dried it, but the stupid phone wouldn't stop singing. It wasn't singing nicely anymore. Now it sounded like a whining cry, so Appa wrapped it in tin foil because Mama still said we weren't going to waste a buck. He put it in the freezer. After a long time singing poorly slower and slower, it stopped.

Much later Appa took the phone out, thinking the problem resolved. As it defrosted, it sung sick-like "London Bridge" again. Appa said, "This is more like a bridge under troubled water."

My parents laughed till they cried, and I got away with my crime. That time.

I continued to do mischievous things and continued to be put in time-out. I angstly hated being prohibited from moving. It was an impossible situation, and I cried real tears.

Finally, Mama and Appa had enough of my mischief. Mama cried, and Appa said, "I can't do this anymore." He grabbed his wallet and keys and walked out of the house.

A few hours later Appa came home with a bag. He found a special place called "herbal store" and bought pills to calm my hyperactivity. I liked them. They were yummy. They improved me a little too.

Something else I enjoyed was the big trampoline. It got some energy out. My siblings would ask, "Wanna go jump-jump?" And I would speed outside like a gust of wind, but I was trapped by the safety fence Appa put up. My siblings could step over it. They lifted me over and set me down, and I ran to the "jump-jump." Someone had to lift me onto it.

When I jumped, I didn't get much momentum because I was tiny and didn't weigh very much. But when my siblings jumped, I flew high in the air and laughed like a hyena! When they stopped, I used sign language for "more-more" and even said it in English now.

But my skin started breaking down. I was allergic, so Appa put his extra-tall tube socks on my arms and legs. They covered my arms to my shoulders and legs to my hips. I looked like a sock monkey!

Every day I asked to go "jump-jump" and ran out the door. But Mama caught up with me. She signed and said, "Pay attention. First socks, then jump-jump."

This is how I learned to do things in a certain order—"pay attention, first" and "then." My brain wasn't giving right messages, but this taught me steps and eventually helped me understand actions have consequences. But this was a long, hard journey.

FYI:
(p) Tuning fork
(q) Lisch nodule: "beauty mark" on the eye's iris

| 5 |

Testing, Testing! 1, 2, 3!

"He was so tiny and presented so many problems to his parents." —E. B. White [10]

I had a toy kitchen with play food, plates, cups, forks, knives, and spoons. I didn't understand forks and knives because in Korea I used fingers, a different kind of spoon, and training chopsticks.

One day Mama moved my toy kitchen, table, chairs, and other fun things out of the laundry room and into our real kitchen. This didn't make me happy. I liked things in a certain order—even if that order was messed up.

I also didn't like plans changing. Usually after breakfast, I took my yummy herb pills. Then I got dressed and brushed my teeth with help, and Mama combed my hair. Then I put my shoes on, and we went outside on nice days. I wanted to jump-jump or go down the road on my trike.

On our walks, Mama kept me at the side of the road and said, "Side of the road." I learned what that meant because she steered me there. It was a long walk, but I loved it very much.

When we made it to the creek, I got off my trike and said, "Hi, ckeek!" Then I crossed the road and said, "Hi, ckeek!" I didn't speak

English yet, but Mama said "Hi, creek!" the first time we went on that adventure, so I was like a little parrot. This was my pattern.

I wanted to stay there, but Mama always said, "Let's go tell the mailbox 'boo.'" I turned my trike around, said "Bye, ckeek," headed back to our house, and stopped at the mailbox. Mama opened it, she picked me up, and I said "boo" into it. It echoed, and I laugh joyfully. Then I slammed the mailbox door closed and ran up to the house.

I waited for Mama who was sluggish after long walks. We went into the house, and I took my shoes off and put them by the door.

So this day, when Mama moved my toy kitchen, was different than my usual routine. I ran to get my shoes, and Mama said, "Ani. No." Then she signed "wait." I stomped my foot like a little general, but I don't know if generals actually do that. I despised that "wait" sign. I became out-of-sync—like a top that spins fine then goes cockeyed.

Knock-knock. Who's there? I ran to the door. So did the dog. Mama signed and said "wait," grabbed the dog, and took her to the laundry room. Appa came into the dining room (where our front door was), picked me up, and opened the door.

In came this random grandma-like lady, and Appa led her into the kitchen. He put me down. I ran around trying to get out, but I was blocked in.

The lady sat down. *Is she a threat? Why is she here? The house has been breached!* This was my safety zone. She was a stranger—like Mama was at the airport when I came to "Amicka."

The lady talked with my parents as I pulled out toy foods from my kitchen. Her voice was like a lullaby. It soothed the savage beast—me. She scribbled in a notebook with her pen.

I spotted my Play-Doh, grabbed it, and handed the green can to Mama. She opened it, pulled the doh out, and put it on my little table. I tried to make a snake, but it kept breaking. I threw it on the floor. Mama said, "Ani," and pointed to it. That meant I needed to pick it up. Mama made a Play-Doh ball, put it in my hand, and helped me press that on the pieces on the floor. Like magic, the Play-Doh pieces stuck to the ball, and cleanup was fun.

When the Play-Doh was in the can, I said, "Bye, Pay-Doh." Mama set it aside. Appa put the basket with my little cars on the table, and I picked a green car to show the lady. She smiled and said words that made me think she liked it. Then I laid my head on the table and lined up the cars like always.

The lady said a lot of things, and my parents did too. Then she closed her notebook, stood up, and said goodbye, and I said, "Bye." I knew that word because I always said goodbye to the creek. Then she left.

Another day Mama brought me to a big building with an elevator. She pushed a button, the door opened, and we went in it. I saw lots of buttons. I loved them profusely. My hands were everywhere on them, and they lighted up as the door closed.

Mama grabbed my hands and said "Ani. No." She pushed Cancel. Then she held both my hands in one of hers and pushed just one button.

When the door opened, Mama held my hand as we went into a room with a little table with a little chair on one side and a big chair on the other side. I sat in the little one. Mama pulled another chair near me to keep me in mine.

A lady came in with a Korean man. She shook Mama's hand while the Korean man bowed. He sat next to us, and the lady sat in the big chair across from me. I didn't pay particular attention to the Korean man.

The lady set up a spiral-bound book and flipped to the first page. She pointed to a picture of a car and waited for me to answer. I did, and the Korean man said something. She turned the page and pointed to a flower. I said a word, and he shrugged. The lady flipped to the next page. I got excited. "Chimmy!" But the Korean man shook his head and said, "I do not understand his Korean."

I had other evaluations that showed I needed help to catch up. I was approved to attend preschool special education summer school.

Appa, Mama, and me visited it. I was riding in my car seat and saw a green building. We went inside! Little kids were having a good time.

Appa and Mama each held one of my hands. Appa could hold mine without me breaking away, but Mama couldn't. She always had me hold her pointer finger then grasped hold of my wrist.

All these new things put my system into overdrive, but my parents kept hold of me until we got to the gym. There were big and small balls, spinning things, tubes to crawl through! A guy and lady asked if I wanted to play. Appa and Mama gave me my freedom. I ran around like a wild child enjoying everything. I had lots of fun! I flapped my hands, yelled, and laughed maniacally.

When the fun was over, we left and got in the van. I signed "more," said it in English too, and pointed to the green building; but we drove away. I looked back, and it was shrinking. I hoped I could go there again before it disappeared. Then I fell asleep.

Mama bought me a new backpack—bigger than my Korean one. She shortened the straps to fit this little rascal. She put in snack and juice box, little notebook with my name on it, and change of clothes.

The day came for my awaited adventure. Mama took me to the green building we visited before. I yelled, "Gheen!" and clapped. I tried to take my seatbelt off, but Mama said, "No. Wait." (I understood short words in English now.) The building got bigger as we drove closer—big enough for me to go into it.

Mama took me to my classroom and said goodbye. She bent down to hug me, but I was off like a bullet. Then I stopped in my tracks and looked back worriedly.

Mama said, "I'll be back. I promise." Then she left but kept her promise.

During six-week summer school, I did many fun and interesting things, and this helped me learn. I also had therapies and wore a weighted vest. They brushed me with a special kind of brush, did joint compression on my legs and arms, rolled me in a rug like a burrito and rolled me about. I loved that!

They also laid me on my stomach on a huge ball. They held my feet, rolled the ball forward, and made me "fly" like an airplane—my body stiff and straight, my head lifted, and my arms stretched out. I looked like a "T"—a lowercase "t." This legit terrified me. But I got used to it, and my body strength increased.

By end of summer school, I could count to one hundred forward and backward, and I was speaking full-on English—a tiny not quite three-and-a-half-year-old genius!

| 6 |

Foiled Plans

"The LORD is on my side; I will not fear:
what can man do unto me?" Psalm 118:6 [11]

August 1996. I wasn't giving a care and just being myself. My only sister (I call her "Sissy" here) went to work at a camp but didn't come home. My three-and-a-half-year-old brain thought people go to camp and don't come back.

My brothers were in their rooms. I was in the living room with Appa and Mama. I couldn't be in there alone because I jammed things in the VCR. I played with my little cars and watched a cartoon movie.

Knock-knock. Who's there? Mama went to the door and called Appa, but I was glued but not with glue to the cartoon. Appa and Mama didn't come back. Then I heard Mamma talk loud.

I jumped up, grabbed some cars, and ran into the dining room. Mama picked me up and put me on her lap next to Appa at the table. A strange lady sat on the other side.

I put my cars on the table and lined them up. I looked at Mama, but she didn't notice I did a good job. Her face was wet, and her lip quivered.

Stephen came downstairs, peeked around the corner, and smiled.

Appa with serious tone said, "Stephen, go upstairs, and stay there."

Stephen unsmiled and obeyed.

The strange lady said Sissy's name and something about "charges." Then she pushed papers across the table. I tried to grab them, but Appa stopped me.

Then Appa told the strange lady to leave.

She went out the door.

One day another lady came, but I knew her. She visited before. She was "Adoption-Case-Worker." I liked her very much. She watched me play, talked to me, and laughed when I acted silly. But this time she just talked and sad-smiled at me.

Appa held me on his lap, and I scribbled in a coloring book while my parents talked with her. Then I laid the crayons like a long train. I looked up at Appa. *Does he like my train?*

Appa patted my back.

Then Mama folded her arms and laid her head on them.

Adoption-Case-Worker put her hand on Mama's back and gently patted her. Then she pointed to my coloring book. "Min Soo, do you like to color?"

"Gheen cayon!" I said in full-on English and showed her because I was so clever.

Adoption-Case-Worker stood up and rubbed the top of my hair. Then she gave my parents hugs and said she would pray. I knew "pray." Then she left.

Our home wasn't the same anymore. I said, "Sissy camp." And Mama said "no" and cried. Sometimes Appa and Mama went to "lawyer," and my big same-brothers watched me. They let me play with their gerbils.

Then Mama packed suitcases and told me awful news. "Stephen's going to camp."

Sissy went to camp. Now I'll never see Stephen again. I asked every day, "Stephen camp?" and fretted, but one day we picked him up. I jabbered all the way home and nearly drove him nuts. I was just extremely happy!

Glenn and Karen were family friends. We did things together. Mama took me and Stephen bowling with Karen and her kids. I threw the bowling ball in the air, and everybody scattered like bugs. It landed in another lane.

Sometimes, when Appa and Mama did "lawyer" or "court," Karen came with her kids. We had fun. Karen always smiled and baked things.

Another lady arrived with suitcases. Mama said she was from far, far away, and she came on an airplane. I was familiar with that experience.

Mama showed me a picture in the book my family sent to Korea. This lady matched the one in our house. This was "aunt."

Aunt Carolyn played with me and took me to McDonald's. We had great fun! Then she took my brothers to a movie and dinner out.

I was home with Appa and Mama when the excitement began, but it really started at church that morning.

I was in my Sunday School class at the table scribbling. I glanced up, and Sissy was next to me. I said, "Sissy camp." She said, "No," but I kept repeating it. I looked down at my paper and up again, but she disappeared—like a magic trick.

When Mama came to get me, she held me tight and walked fast. I said, "Sissy camp," but Mama said, "No," and we hurried to the van.

After nap time, I played in the living room. Appa and Mama finished watching people singing joyful songs on a video.[r] It sounded like *Gaither's Pond*,[12] but the people weren't animals. Then Appa started a cartoon movie for me.

Suddenly, lights flashed outside our big window. I ran over and saw a police car. Then number two and three came with lights flashing!

It was the most exciting thing! Appa brought Stephen a toy police car from Korea. It made noise and flashed lights too, but I broke it.

Mama said, "What in the world!"

Appa said, "This can't be happening!" He raced out the front door. So did I. *Appa is taking me to see the police cars!*

Mama came out and scooped me up in her arms.

There was a lady from Sissy's school (I knew that because sometimes we went there). Then Sissy got out of the lady's van.

Appa told Mama, "Get Min out of sight!" Mama ran inside with me around the kitchen corner. *We are going to play hide-n-seek!* I played that with my brothers. Sometimes I fell asleep before they found me.

Mama patted my back faster and faster, bounced me a little, and whispered, "It's okay, Min. It's okay." You're not supposed to talk during hide-n-seek.

Afterwhile, Mama set me down. I ran to look outside, but the police cars were gone. I was sad.

Then Aunt Carolyn came back from the fun time with my brothers—all laughing and happy until they saw Appa and Mama and stopped dead in their tracks.

I didn't understand until I grew that my parents learned Sissy was in class with me. They asked her to come talk in the afternoon. She agreed, but she brought police and boxes instead, took her stuff, and didn't say anything.

Sissy moved far away to live with a bad man (who used to be at her school). He went to another court to own her and tried to get me too, but his plan got foiled.

Sometimes I ask about my sister. My parents talk a little then say, "This isn't easy to talk about." So I stop.

My sister broke family roots. She promised to sing to me, but she broke her promise. I want to shake my fists and say, "How could you rip us up so badly and make me boil over!"

When Mama and Appa did "lawyer" now, Aunt Carolyn took care of me. She stayed until leaves fell off the trees.

I like stomping on leaves! They go "crunch." Sometimes Stephen and me would jump in piles of leaves and bury ourselves.

Lovely Mourning Dove,   *September 1996*

"Ooah-ooh-oo-oo" is your song—dependable as the sunrise.

I wait on our large front stoop with our new son. I can't take my eyes off him. Two reasons. First, if I do, he's off like a flash! Secondly, he's such a beautiful gift.

When he's awake, Min's never still nor quiet except when he runs out in the morning to await his preschool bus, freezes in place, and listens because he believes you're speaking to him. He never tires of your repetitious song, much like he is—always the same. Predictable. He speaks your language and answers, "Hoo-OO-hoo-hoo," awaits your reply, and answers again. Then he hears his bus rumble toward our home.

Min and I head down, hand-in-hand, and wait until the bus stops and opens its doors. Then he boards. When he's seat-belted in, the bus pulls away. I wave every day. I'm predictable too. Sometimes he looks my way, sometimes not because his mind jumps to the next thing. But I wave anyway.

Then I head up to the house and park myself on our bench. The cool morning air helps clear my mind, but my heart's still breaking.

I contemplate your "song," Mourning Dove, which resonates from your chest. We're minus a child to send off to school—our songbird who's taken flight. This is why I've adopted your song—because I can't find mine. It's a moaning from my chest also.

The beautiful son I waved to, doesn't understand. He sees her picture and words in the book we sent him—"I will be your big sister when you come to live with us. I like to sing. I can teach you songs. I can't wait until you get here."

Now we're a home of two sorrows because our little son may be removed. Can we lose two children without dying inside?

We have no song. Only your sad one. "Ooah-ooh-oo-oo." Do you cry, too,
when you "sing?"

With pain's "song" inside me,
this broken mother

When Mama took me to my bus now, she scanned the area because the strange lady (who came in August) wanted to know where us boys went to school. My parents wouldn't tell her.

But then I missed school because I got sick with a fever. Mama took me to the kids' doctor who was very grouchy this time—not fun like before. Mama was quiet driving home, and I heard her sniffle.

One day my big same-brothers came home from school sad-looking and told my parents the strange lady questioned them, so Appa sat waiting for Stephen.

When I heard his bus, I ran to the door. Me and the dog always did that, but Appa said and signed, "Wait." I wasn't good at "wait."

When Stephen came in, he cried and sat on Appa's lap.

"Did the CPS (r) lady come to your school too?"

"Yeah." He wiped his eyes and nose on his sleeve. "She asked me stuff. I told her you're good parents."

Then Appa and Stephen talked about his day. I waited because sometimes Stephen played jump-jump with me after snack. Not today.

Stephen said, "Min, I must teach you a new game."

I hated plans changing, but "new game" sounded okay.

After snack, we hiked far in our back woods. We found good hiding places and practiced in case monsters came (like the strange lady or bad man). I needed to be still and quiet. That challenged me to infinity, but Stephen said, "It's super important! If you do good, I'll play rolling Rock Monster with you."

I loved playing that! Stephen rolled all over the trampoline, and I jumped over him. That was as much fun as eating rice for lunch, which was the very best thing.

Everything seemed fun to me, except Mama cried, and Appa didn't sing or play guitar anymore.

After too-many-sleeps to count, we got vacation from school. But I started counting sleeps right away because I loved school.

Christmas was coming! Karen visited with her kids and decorated our Christmas tree because Mama said, "I just can't." I helped Karen, but it was hard for me.

Then I got a package from Omma with an ornament. Mama helped me hang it on the tree. The cat climbed our tree. That made me laugh. The cat didn't like me much. I don't know why.

Sunday afternoons we went to Cambodian church. The people looked like me and treated me like one of their own. I was in Mama's Sunday School class. Appa taught bigger kids. At church dinners, I ran wild with the kids. They were good at "imp" too.

My birthday arrived! I had a party with the Cambodian kids and at the green preschool. Two birthdays, but I was still four.

I started to stutter. My teachers said my brain was learning English so fast that my speech jumbled up. I also was still wild and got hurt.

I speeded my trike across our big high-up stoop. I forgot to stop with my feet and flew through the air, laughing maniacally—until my forehead landed on the sidewalk.

Mama scooped me up, and we ran to get an ice pack. I cried so much and got a lump called "goose egg." I fought Mama from holding ice on it, but she said, "Min, you must keep it on until I finish singing."

Mama sang me a counting song, and I whimpered the numbers with her. It took many numbers. I didn't mind then because I loved numbers, and I'm an excellent counter.

Next day was picture day at preschool. The egg got smaller overnight, and—like magic—it changed colors. Mama wrote a note to school and put make-up on the egg.

I climbed the back of the recliner. It let go. I fell backwards and split my head on the fireplace bricks and needed stitches.

Mama said not to get hurt again because the hospital only had three flavors of popsicles, so we shouldn't go back anymore. That made sense to me.

Appa and Mama kept a pretty room for Sissy in case she came home. But she didn't.

To the Bruised Reed and Smoldering Wick,   *April-August 1997*

Our adoption case worker received a letter from our daughter, saying she wasn't abused and wants Min to be adopted by us. But we were put on trial for the charges anyway, so Min couldn't "become ours" until the court made their decision. He'd been with us eleven months by then—now fifteen. How could we lose him!

Many testified on our behalf—including AIAA's state supervisor. All seemed to go well, and our lawyer said it would end soon. But it didn't. The "bad man," a minister, reported another false claim, saying we abused Min. The battle continued in court.

Your promise carried us. "Ye shall not fear them: for the Lord your God he shall fight for you." Deuteronomy 3:22 [13]

Now four months later, we receive the court's decision. "Charges unfounded." Yet the law states our case remains unsealed for ten years after our daughter's eighteenth birthday—2008 (when four-year-old Min is fifteen). Any false accusation reopens this nightmare.

Outside the halls of justice, the "bad man" continued attacking. From early on, he'd been in cahoots with our pediatrician who illegally gave him private records. He gossiped to our support base and local churches, recruited others, and threatened our mission board.

We could tolerate no more and begged our mission director to relocate us.

"Brian and Sarah, we will," he said, "but when you leave, you'll go with heads held high."

God called us to minister to children and train others to do so. Gossip shut down nearly everything. We sunk into deep depression, and our support base collapsed.

Brian took extra employment to keep us afloat and pay legal debts.

During school hours, I worked for an elderly friend who encouraged me.

"You two are incredibly strong."

"We don't feel that way," I answered.

"Well, it's good you have Min," she said.

"How? He's 24/7."

"He makes you get up in the morning and put your feet on the floor."

"I guess." I finished my jobs and went home.

The house was deadly quiet. Suddenly, my mostly silent husband spoke. "A bruised reed God won't break, and a smoldering wick He won't snuff out."

"Where's that found?"

"It's from Isaiah 42:3. We're bruised but not broken. And a smoldering wick can reignite. God isn't done with us yet."

> Carrying the Gospel Light,
> Bruised-but-not-broken

FYI:

[r] Gaither Homecoming video

[s] Child Protective Services

| 7 |

Happy Adoption Day!

"When a judge says you're adopted, you're not borrowed,
and you're not just visiting ... adoption is for always."
—Linda Walvoord Girard [14]

Surprise! One of my Korean foster brothers and his friend visited me. I was supercalifragilisticly excited and wild as I did numerous fun activities with him and his friend (who videotaped me). Foster-Brother gave me new clothes with fun pictures.

He said, "Min Soo does not seem to remember me."

Mama answered. "I'm not sure, but he is enjoying your visit."

Foster-Brother wrote in my memory book as tears ran down his face.

Then we went out on the stoop and waved goodbye. The dog came too.

The car got smaller and smaller as they drove away until I thought I could pick it up and bring it back. Then it disappeared.

The next day I was angst. Stephen was going to camp.

Mama set me on her lap and stroked my forehead upward, just like Mrs. Choi comforted me in Korea. "Don't worry. Stephen will return soon."

One more sleep and summer school started. I wore my new clothes from Foster-Brother. When I came home, I told Mama, "I cried at school. When is Stephen coming home?"

"When the bank says 8."

I loved the bank sign's digital numbers. I was an excellent counter, and the numbers were getting higher.

And on 8, Stephen came home, but he wasn't as happy as me because I broke his snow globe. That ended us sharing a room.

My parents painted the under-stairs space like Noah's Ark and added animal-shaped letters. My mattress, favorite books, and stuffed animals moved in. Appa put a safety gate across the doorway so my animals couldn't escape. During the day, I ran wild and played in my toy area and outside, but I loved my new "ark" room. It felt safe.

At the next visit with Adoption-Case-Worker, she said, "Let's get this little guy adopted!"

Mama and Appa smiled so big.

My parents tried to explain adoption, but it confused four-and-a-half-year-old me. I thought I was Hampshire family, so I only understood we would go someplace all dressed up and become who I already was.

So November 14ᵗʰ, 1997, we got ready. Appa drove down icy hills, but we arrived at the courthouse.

My parents requested a judge-friend of Appa's for my adoption, and he got that assignment. He was a little person, so me and the judge had things in common. We both had disabilities and were chosen.

In the courtroom, the judge asked Appa to introduce us all. The judge asked questions, and Mama and Appa answered, "Yes." Then the judge asked, "What will your new son's name be?"

Appa said, "Benjamin David Hampshire, your Honor."

The judge especially liked my new middle name. It matched his. My first name was chosen because my parents picked a Bible name with Min in it, and I owned it already four-and-a-half years. They would call me Min as long as I liked being called that.

Also, Benjamin meant important son. That was me! I belonged. No more losing parents. And my middle name was chosen because King David invited Mephibosheth to be family and sit at his table—just like me! Adopted and sitting at the Hampshire table.

In Korea, my last name was Kim because that was my birth mother's name, and I was illegitimate. Now my name was Hampshire. My parents cared about me and loved me, and I was legal too.

From God's way of looking, I always was important, valued, legitimate—even when I was inside my birth mother. I always was heavenly important. From the beginning of time, God made a plan for me, so I figured I wasn't a sin after all. How could I be a sin if God had a plan for me? God hates sin, but He loves me.

I now was adopted, but later I would be adopted again.

At the end of the court time, a lady took our picture standing around the judge. Then we went out into the cold to celebrate.

We went to a big restaurant. I ate until I groaned and held my belly. I got gifts—a USA musical bear and *Happy Adoption Day* book.[15] Everyone got tiny bears with USA flags on them. A great day! I got adopted, but the best part was we ate out!

Back at the green preschool I had an aide full-time because I pushed kids, threw stuff, shouted, and ran out of the room randomly. I was extremely apologetic. I told my teachers and parents I tried to be good, but I repeated these actions.

This puzzled my parents. *Why isn't he learning right ways to act?* Here I lived with them for a year and a half and was all jumbled up. When I was touched gently, I said, "Ouch!"

This frustrated my parents, but for me it was pain.

Also, my ears heard high pitches other people couldn't hear—like "wheee-wheee-wheee" of lights and some electronics, so I hit my ears over and over, yelled, and ran wild.

At my preschool, the grown-ups took me to the gym to get some energy out of me. They rolled me in a rug and pressed on my joints to calm me. My aide learned rubbing a fist down my spine helped—only down, not up, but it didn't last long.

They brushed my arms and legs with a special soft brush. That made me feel myself come together. My parents did this too, but I broke out with rashes because my nerves got agitated from my NF1. Then I picked at the rashes and made sores, so brushing stopped.

Sometimes my nose didn't work right either. When I smelled rubber tires burning or a skunk, I said, "That smells like Mama's lasagna." That made people laugh but not Mama.

My mouth was a nightmare. My parents wanted me to try new foods, like mashed potatoes. I didn't want to, but they said I must have a small no-thank-you helping. I gagged profusely and cried. I hardly ever cried, so crying over mashed potatoes made my parents wonder, *why is he crying over something easy to swallow?*

But I thought, w*hy are they making me eat this when my tongue doesn't know what to do?* None of us understood my tongue couldn't handle different textures and went into spasms. I wasn't trying to be disobedient, but my parents thought I was.

Another thing—I knocked over kids.

My parents said not to be on top of people. On top, on bottom, on the side, above, below, next to—didn't register, and I couldn't tell where people were in space—like someone close seemed small even if we were the same size.

If a kid was close to me, sometimes I screamed in their ear, made them cry, or hit them. I felt bad because I hurt them. I didn't understand boundaries. I liked having kids around, but it was also very hard because I got agitated and behaved worse. I felt safer alone.

My parents couldn't figure me out. I couldn't either. I was a great challenge to grown-ups who knew how to handle kids like me, so I was impossible to grown-ups who were clueless.

So, this happened at church: I got promoted from nursery class (where a nice lady helped me) to preschool class. Mama and Appa gave the new teacher clues how to handle me—like signing "wait" or "sit." The teacher said those were ways her dog obeyed, but my parents said it worked.

The teacher tried for a while. But a couple months later, she saw Mama and took me to her. She said, "I can't handle him anymore. Please don't bring him back," and she passed me over to Mama.

I'm in major trouble for being thrown out of class. I'm doomed!

Mama scooped me up in her arms and hugged me tight. Tears ran down her face. She walked away—me in her grasp. "Let's go get Appa."

This tight hold felt good, not painful. Safe, so I knew I wasn't in trouble, but I didn't have a clue why not.

Appa spotted us outside his Sunday School room and exited. Mama told him what happened, and Appa said, "We're outta here!" We collected brothers and went home.

I loved getting the mail with my parents and still yelled "boo" into the mailbox. This was hysterical to me. When a letter with Korean stamps arrived, they said, "You have mail from Mrs. Choi. Oh, Omma." I got used to hearing "Mrs. Choi," so I didn't call her Omma anymore, but she would always be the mother of my heart.

Mrs. Choi wrote letters in Korean, and one of her sons translated them into English. She sent unique cards—some pretty, some pop-up, some funny. One Christmas card had Korean carolers on it. One little kid was picking his nose. It was hilarious to me because I did that too.

The Christmas after my adoption, Mrs. Choi sent a special card and note:

"Merry Christmas ... Congratulations on Min Soo's adoption. Thank you for your letter and doll [1] which are very precious for us. We will keep them forever not to forget your kindness. We will always pray for you and Min Soo. From Choi, Jung Hee—Foster Mother."

This Christmas I understood about Jesus' Birthday. I blew out the candles on the cake. No one wanted to eat it with my spittle sprayed on it. My brothers taught me to wave a paper plate over birthday candles instead of blowing them out. They said, "That's how we do it here."

To Feline-loving Humans: *Christmas 1997*

Late Christmas Eve, gifts appeared under the tree while the small human slept and his siblings spied. I squeezed between the boxes then slept too.

Christmas morning my bigger humans gathered early, waited, ate breakfast, and waited longer. The terror never slept in. Except today. The mom quietly opened his gate.

Finally, he awoke and tore out of his room. I scurried up the tree to avoid getting launched.

To my surprise, the terror plopped on his mom's lap until his dad read a Book, lowered his head, and said, "Amen." I expected havoc, but no. The small human took a box from his mom, pointed to the tag, and said, "M-I-N." Then he opened the gift and played with it. He seemed annoyed when they gave him another.

If the terror would quit giving me flying lessons, he might be worth keeping. After all, he sneaks me treats.

—the family cat with frequent flyer miles

FYI:

[1] Tiny bear with American flag—adoption party favor

| 8 |

The Night Jesus Came to Church

"Who is this God? What is love? Why did God
give away his son?" —Stephanie Fast
(Korean adoptee, miracle survivor)[16]

Until now, I called my parents Appa and Mama because Omma taught me those words from the special book my family sent to Korea. My brothers always called them Mom and Dad. I was clever and figured out Appa was Dad and Mama was Mom, so I began calling them that.

This was 1998. I became five years old. My NF1 didn't change, but I was often sick with colds and ear infections. I also had very weak coughing, so my parents laid me belly-down across their laps and paddled my back to get lung-boogers out so I wouldn't get seriously sick.

I missed lots of school days. Home was fun, but I always asked when I could go back to school. My parents said "in two sleeps" if that's how many it was or however many it would be.

I graduated from the green preschool. Mom and Dad took me to kindergarten open house at Stephen's school. I was happy to be with him, but now he went to a different building. I couldn't catch up to him.

Church advertised Vacation Bible School with "Veggie Tales!" [17] I liked Bob and Larry and was excited. Stephen was too. Mom would be my aide, but then she said sorry because the church banished us.

Stephen pouted. I did too because I copied him. But I stopped when Mom played a DVD, so I saw Bob and Larry anyway.

Dad called a family meeting and told us we quit church. He said, "From now on we'll do church at home." So that's what we did.

Time to start school! I went on the special ed bus to morning half-day kindergarten. I had a teacher and one-on-one aide. My aide met me at the bus because I arrived all wound up. Then we went to the office to push heavy boxes back and forth or the You & Me Center for activities to calm me for my day.

I had many colds. My aide wrote a note home and asked Mom if I could wear pants with pockets for my tissues. Mom made sure I was prepared. The next day my aide wrote home: "I cracked up when I saw Min in overalls! We didn't run out of pockets all morning!"

Mom worked extra jobs now. When I got home from school, I went with her when she did outside work, but I stayed home with Dad when Mom wallpapered. She couldn't get down the ladder fast enough to keep up with me.

Then something weird happened. A girl came to our house with a boy. I asked who she was, and Mama said, "Your sister."

"I have a sister?" I didn't remember having one.

We had a party because Sissy was marrying this boy far away. I got to stay up late until the other family members left.

Then I went to sleep. When I woke up, Sissy and the boy were gone. So I had a sister before, and she was gone; then I had one again, and she was gone.

We didn't go many places since we went through trials, so it was great fun when we went to Glenn and Karen's house.

Dustin's Rat,   *Autumn of 1998*

We're very sorry for all that happened in your owner's bedroom while we enjoyed a visit downstairs. When we arrived home and received your owner's inflamed e-mail, we were shocked!

Rat, your owner and his parents had every right to be terribly angry. So much cleanup that late at night! By the way, did it take long to find you?

We confronted Min. His explanation? He put you with the guinea pigs. Then he worried you might eat them. He picked up the guinea pig cage to dump you back into yours.

Min lost hold of the whole shebang! You and the guinea pigs escaped. As you scurried about, he grabbed handfuls of cage litter and threw it at you, thinking you'd stop. Of course, that didn't work.

Then Min turned his attention to the fish. We're sorry again because (from Min's description) we're pretty sure the fish are "no longer with us."

Min apologized to Dustin and his parents, Glenn and Karen. Then he asked, "Can I go upstairs and see the animals next time because I said sorry?"

"No!" Karen answered emphatically.

"When can I?"

She fished for an answer. "When you're eight years old!"

Min's countenance dropped. He turned to us and asked, "How many sleeps is that?"

Something like 1,000."

So, Rat, good news! You're protected for the rest of your natural life. When Min turns eight, you won't need a cage, if you catch our drift.

With sympathy,

not proud parents

When leaves turned colors and fell, we had another family meeting. Dad told us it wasn't good we weren't in church.

Mom said, "I don't trust churches anymore."

"There's one far up the road where we know people we trust. How 'bout we just visit?"

We voted to try.

The next Sunday we got ready and drove a long way.

Dad pointed. "This is it."

I looked out and saw McDonald's. I got excited and yelled, "McDonald's Church!" So I always called it that because we decided to go there—not McDonald's. The church.

My parents told Pastor Bruce they had a son—me—with many concerns who some people couldn't handle.

Pastor Bruce explained, if God brought someone with needs, the church must meet the needs. He said, "Your son will be welcomed. My wife will be his Sunday School teacher, and she'll love him."

Mrs. Kathy did love me! I was still full imp, but she smiled and laughed when I was there.

One Sunday Mrs. Kathy made soup. When Mom brought me into class, I sniffed. It smelled wretched!

Mom said, "Smells good."

Mrs. Kathy said, "We're having vegetable soup. The lesson's on Jacob and Esau, and this is our illustration."

Mom told Mrs. Kathy I probably wouldn't eat it.

I didn't like vegetables, but I ate some because at home my parents said, "Vegetables give you gas." I thought gas was funny, so I ate them for the sound effects.

When Mom picked me up, Mrs. Kathy surprised her with news I ate the soup. "Min told us he likes vegetable soup because it gives him gas!"

Mom wasn't sure what to do because we were new, but Mrs. Kathy was laughing, so Mom let her guard down.

Dad stopped singing when Sissy left. Now he sang in the choir. And once in a while we got McDonald's after, so we had a great church and fries with that!

My birthday–March 9th. I turned six-years-old.

Soon it was Easter. McDonald's Church practiced a special program, and Dad sang in it. My big same-brothers acted in it too. Mom took Stephen and me. She sat on the end of the aisle so I couldn't escape.

The play was called "He's Alive," [18] about Jesus' life at the end. It was so real to me. I felt like I was there. When it was time for Jesus to die, He came up the aisle looking all beat up, and he wore a crown of thorns. Jesus carried a long, heavy part of the cross. He struggled extremely.

I jumped from my seat and wanted to get past Mom, but she grabbed the back of my shirt. "You must stay in your seat."

"But I need to help him! He's having a really bad time!"

Mom was moved by my actions, but she said, "We can't help him right now," and placed me in my seat. She put her arm around me.

My eyes were glued on Jesus—not like real glue—and I got emotional. At the front of the church, soldiers took that long, heavy part of the cross off Jesus.

I couldn't see what was happening and worried. I jumped up and stood on my chair. Mom held my pants loop so I wouldn't fall.

Soldiers nailed that heavy part of the cross right-angle to the other part. They hammered loud. *Clank, clank, clank, clank, clank, clank.*

The background music sounded ominous. *Something bad is about to happen.*

Then they lifted the cross and "*thud!*" Jesus was hanging on it.

Mom sat me on her lap.

I buried my head in Mom's chest and sobbed, "I can't believe He did this for me."

Mom sobbed too. She wrapped her arms around me tight and whispered, "He'll be all right. I promise."

The church turned dark. This didn't look like "all right" to me. Then there was thunder! Super loud! And lightning! I covered my ears and closed my eyes because I was afraid of storms. Mom kept holding me tight.

The music changed, and lights came on. I saw an empty cross. *Where did Jesus go?*

Then Jesus walked in the side door with His Arms stretched out and showed us nail marks in His Hands.

I was shocked! Jesus was alive and well! I was so happy!

The people up front sang Jesus was risen and Heaven was open now for anyone who accepted Jesus as their Savior. What wonderful news!

In May at McDonald's Church I was dedicated. Pastor Bruce and Mrs. Kathy were in front, and my parents brought me up there.

Dad carried me because I was wild—throwing myself back and flapping my hands in the air. Mrs. Kathy tried to hold back laughing. She failed.

Then Pastor Bruce asked if my parents promised to raise me for the Lord spiritually.

My parents answered, "We will."

Pastor Bruce addressed the church-goers. He told them they needed to pray for our family, encourage us, and be like Jesus to us.

Then Pastor Bruce put his hand on my back because Dad still held me, and he prayed my parents would keep their promise and the church-goers would too. He also prayed for the day I would ask Jesus into my life.

Then Pastor Bruce opened a little box, took out a small book, and read. I heard my name and tried to grab it. Pastor Bruce finished and gave me a little blue Bible. I couldn't read yet, but I loved owning this little Bible and taking it to church. I loved things that fit 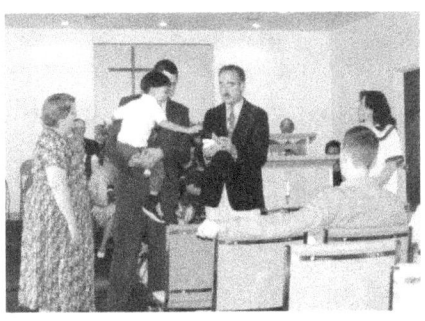 in my pocket and carried it like a treasure.

At my young age, I knew how important God was.

I knocked on Stephen's bedroom door.

He said, "Come in."

I plopped on the bed with Stephen and crisscrossed my legs. I asked him to pray with me so I could ask Jesus into my life. Stephen explained in words I understood—that I needed to tell Jesus I was sorry for my sins, thank Him for dying on the cross and washing away my sins, and invite Him into my life.

I remembered that because the Easter play sparked my mind to realize what it all meant. I knew Jesus didn't stay dead. He came alive three days later. It was prophesied.

Jesus is still alive—both in Heaven and in hearts of people who ask Him in. God isn't a dictator. He gives the choice of accepting Him or not.

I asked Jesus to come into my life. I was both sad and happy. The sad part was Jesus died. The happy part was He came alive so I could ask Him into my life. I was adopted again—this time into the Lord's family!

Then Stephen took me to Dad. "Min has something to tell you."

I told Dad, "I asked Jesus into my life."

He was happy and gave me a hug. Then he had me sit and tell him what I did. I told him. He realized I understood and became a Christian that day.

When Mom got home from working at her friend's, Dad told her what I did, and Mom was happy too.

My grown-up self understands the Holy Spirit spoke to my soul. He could do that because my soul isn't disabled. Even though I'm permanently mentally disabled until death, God offered His free gift of salvation to me. That makes me astonished!

| 9 |

Missions Accomplished

*"... everybody should have a purpose in life and
pursue it faithfully." —Lucy Maud Montgomery* [19]

We wrote back and forth with Mrs. Choi, and she sent packages
with Korean items reminding me of my life there. Mrs. Choi always
remembered my birthday with something special. She loved me and
never forgot me. When I would become Korean-American, my parents
would let her know my mission was completed.

In the late spring, a letter came saying I was going to be
naturalized. That meant become a kid-citizen without taking tests due
to my age. The ceremony would be at the zoo. My family thought that
was hysterical and fitting because I was such a sock monkey, always
jumping even without a trampoline. I was bombarded with joy about a
day at the zoo!

The day arrived. My family, Aunt Carolyn, and Glenn and Karen
joined hundreds of people there.

I noticed numerous dark-haired children—not just me. All forty-
seven overseas adoptees, their families, and guests gathered for the
ceremony.

Dad held me up in his arms so I could see everything. There were speeches, saying the Pledge of Allegiance, and singing "The Star-Spangled Banner."

Then we were asked questions. We were supposed to raise our right hand and say "I will," but I didn't know which hand that was. Dad helped me, and I answered, "I will." Then the crowd applauded. Some people cried tears of joy. Everybody smiled!

A man gave me an American flag and a certificate.

I was now American. After that, we wandered around the zoo as long as we wanted. Then we went home and had a party. It was a wonderful day.

The next month the phone rang, and Dad clicked away on the computer. A picture of a baby showed up on the monitor. It didn't have much hair, so I figured it was a boy.

Dad said, "Min, you're an uncle." He printed copies of the baby for us. We smiled that day. I took my picture to summer school for show and tell.

When I started first grade, Sissy and the boy visited with the baby. I wanted to help feed him, so Mom had me sit on the couch because babies are fragile. I got ready, and Sissy placed him on my lap.

I yelled. The baby screamed, then I screamed more, and he screamed louder. That didn't go well, but now I think it's a riot. Once he calmed, I fed him.

Happy New Year 2000! Everyone celebrated a new century. For me it all seemed the same, except one day my parents announced big news. We would leave New York and find a new location.

I wasn't happy because I liked where I was. We didn't know where to move. Dad said, "We'll pack then see where God takes us." That's what we did, and we prayed God would deliver us to a new start.

Dad and Mom met with their BCM[20] mission boss and asked about going to Kentucky. He said there was an urgent need. We prayed.

I turned seven. I had headaches and got glasses. I kept pulling them on and off and losing them. It nearly drove my school aide crazy. One time I bent them badly and fixed them myself. That didn't go well.

Then the time came for my first MRI. (It was delayed because of all my family went through.) Barney the Dinosaur [21] went with me. I don't know if he liked being there. I had this test to see if there were signs of neurofibromatosis type 1 (NF1) in my brain.

Because I was squirmy, they sedated me. *Sleep tight. Don't let the needles bite.* I'm glad I slept because the noises would've spooked me. (I know this now because I have had MRIs to-a-galaxy-far-far-away amount.) Parents weren't permitted in the MRI room.

When it was over, I woke up and looked around. No Mom—only a nurse. I began bawling like my heart was broken.

The nurse tried to comfort me but couldn't. She asked another nurse to get Mom.

It seemed like eternity till Mom came. I clung to her and buried my head in her chest, and I gulped weird as I cried.

Mom hugged me tight. "What's the matter? Is something hurting you?"

"I thought you left me."

"No, Min. I wouldn't leave you," Mom cooed like a mother bird. "We'd never leave you."

My adult self understands, when mom said she wouldn't leave me, she at-the-bottom-of-her-heart meant it.

The MRI showed spots nicknamed UBOs—"unidentified bright objects." The doctors said these would disappear when I was older, but now they were signs of NF1 in my extra-terrestrial brain. Before I was an alien to the United States. Now I was out of the solar system.

Back to earth! We decided to visit Kentucky and make a vacation of it.

First out west to visit for the short-haired baby's birthday.

Then we drove to Kentucky and met other BCM missionaries. We took along a small tent to use for us boys to camp out. Mom and Dad slept inside the mission building.

Next, we headed to Pennsylvania Dutch country to meet Uncle Bruce, Aunt Heather, and Grandma for a fun time. Uncle Bruce was treating us.

Some people along our travels gave us a money gift. We bought food and gas. Our money was low, but we didn't know how low because Mom forgot to check.

Then Dad asked Mom to get more out of the envelope we kept under the passenger seat.

Mom pulled it out. "Uh oh. We're down to our last twenty dollars."

Mom and Dad wondered how we would manage until we joined family in Pennsylvania. "Lord, we need Your help."

We had our small tent and no money for a motel. We would be smooshed.

We found a campground in Gettysburg, Pennsylvania. It looked ominous, but it had to do because we weren't meeting family until the next afternoon. We pulled in and got out of the car.

An old man who looked like a skinny Belsnickel (u) walked toward us. We greeted him, and he showed us where to put our tent. Then he said he was having open-heart surgery that week and was petrified he was going to die.

Dad told him about the Lord, and Mom gave him her Bible. We said we would pray for him and that the Bible would comfort him with answers for all his fears.

He thanked us, looked at the Bible, and felt the leather. He had water in his eyes.

Then Dad asked Belsnickel, "How much does a night cost here?"

"Twenty dollars."

Uh oh. We had that much, but then we couldn't eat the next day.

Then Belsnickel said, "But you can stay here for ten dollars because you gave me this beautiful book."

Our prayer was answered. We had enough money for the night and pizza the next day. And Belsnickel? Sometimes you just have to be at a place because God wants you there. Maybe he's in Heaven now. I think that's why we ended up there. (I hope he doesn't mind I called him Belsnickel.)

We enjoyed much fun with our relatives in Pennsylvania—Dutch Wonderland, visiting the Tabernacle display, and best of all we ate at restaurants. Uncle Bruce let me pick anything I wanted!

FYI:
(u) "Crotchety" folklore figure who gave Christmas gifts

| 10 |

The "Eyes" Have It

"He must be a corker of a boy: I hope you are prepared
for the possibility he might turn out a saint."
—C.S. Lewis [22]

When we got home from our trip, my parents and their mission agreed we would go to Kentucky. I was happy because my parents told me the pets were going too! And there was a Chinese restaurant over the mountain!

We decided to stay in New York one more year until my big same-brothers, Nathan and Michael, graduated. Before senior year Michael went to Army boot camp. By now I knew, when someone went to camp, they came back.

I was in second grade. Election year—Bush against Gore for President. We voted in our classroom. Bush won, so I thought it was over. This was the first time I ever voted. It was a huge deal because I became a United States citizen the year before, and you must be a citizen to vote.

During this year I became ommetaphobic—scared of eyes—because in Scooby-Doo [23] I was spooked by culprits who spied through paintings with eyeholes.

I wasn't in the under-the-stairs Noah's ark room anymore because I grew. My new room was big enough for a youth bed, dresser, table and chair for my desk and play. I still had a toy area off the kitchen. My new room was next to that. Mom helped me make my bed and lined up the stuffed animals to keep me company at night.

But every morning the animals faced the wall at the end of my bed. Mom turned them around. Then that night I put them at the end, facing the wall. This went on for a while.

Finally, Mom asked, "Why are you doing this? The animals are your friends."

"I'm scared of their eyes. They stare at me when I'm going to sleep."

After that, Mom put the animals at the end of the bed, facing the wall.

Then I saw "Toy Story," [24] and I knew, when humans slept, the toys came alive. I threw the animals out of my room—over and over. Mom kept putting them back. Finally, I came clean. "I don't trust them. They might turn around and stare at me." After that, the stuffed animals were ordered out of my room by King Me.

Another thing that terrified me was the dentist. On appointment days I was angst at school and still was when Mom picked me up. I had bad teeth troubles. Mom said that if I did good at the dentist, I could have something special for supper.

Dear Tooth Fairy,

Thank you for the shiny quarters you placed under Min's pillow.

Looks like we'll continue a long relationship with you and the dentist, including monthly payments for who-knows-how-long. Min's teeth are THAT BAD. We've tried everything to help him brush better—different flavored toothpastes, toothbrushes that play music or jingle, etc. Yet he fails to grasp hand-with-brush-to-mouth but totally gets finger-in-nose.

Tooth Fairy, are you familiar with a lifeguard's emergency rescue board? The dentist straps our son onto one. Min's immobilized except for his toes, which continuously wiggle like Fred Flintstone's when he's preparing to release his bowling ball down the alley. [25]

Min's eyes dart about, probably sending coded messages for help. He's not quiet—even with a rubber dam in his mouth—and complains in a garbled-muffled mix, sounding like some ancient war cry.

The oh-so-patient dentist uses laughing gas to subdue our son. This helps get the job done. She warns, though, Min's permanent teeth are coming in damaged.

We'd be rich if paid for our coaching during his appointments, but all we earn are more gray hairs. Our standard Min-motivator helps us survive— "If you're very good, you can have rice for supper!"

Tooth Fairy, keep those quarters comin'! Min won't part with them to help pay his bills, so we'll continue printing money in the basement.

Minus the laughing gas,
parents with ink on their fingers

In March 2001 I turned eight. By now we had more boxes ready for Kentucky. My self wanted to take every single little car I owned with me. I worried. Kentucky was far away, and things get tinier when they are that far. *Maybe my cars won't fit in the new house.*

Mom and Dad traveled to find a home and left us with a grand-mother-figure who us boys liked. Two days later our parents called. They found a place to live and told her, "Tell Min our new house is big enough for all his cars." My worries were over!

Nathan and Michael graduated, and Michael left right away for more Army training. He would join us in Kentucky later. My parents were extremely happy about leaving New York. Now we were on our way!

Dear School Notebooks,   *June 2001*

You're the written records to and from Min's one-on-one aides his first three years of elementary school. As we read you, our hearts break, realizing Min's struggles. We're also amazed what's been accomplished with his tremendous challenges. His aides gave their all.

Min briefly talked one aide into letting him "write" his notes home, dictating as she scribed:

"I had a very bad day. Poor Mrs. C., poor Mrs. E., poor Mrs. B., poor Mrs. K, poor cows. —Min"

"I had a good day today. I got playtime and helped clean up ... I went in line when the whistle blew. I didn't yell or make noise. It was a thumbs-up day. —Min"

"I had a good day. I went down the slide, not up. I didn't yell. I had time-out because I didn't listen. Lunch was good! I had another time-out. I yelled and kicked like a baby because I didn't roll a four for math practice. —Min"

"I had a three-thumbs-up day. Can we go to Walmart because W is my favorite letter? I shared glue, scissors, and colored pencils with kids. I walked and sat quietly in the circle. I had really good lunch and ice cream for special treat. —Min"

His aides' sentiments, as each year closed, touched us—

Kindergarten: "Min's added a very special dimension to my life. I'm blessed to witness the work of God through Min's growth. I'll miss him and keep you in my prayers, believing the purpose for which you're created will continue until its completion. —Mrs. C."

First Grade: "I've enjoyed working with Min. Good days far outweighed the bad. By the way, no one understands my kidding like Min does! He looks at me, pauses, and says, 'You're joking, right?' He cracks me up! My husband wondered why I needed to go to bed at 8:00 weeknights this year. —Mrs. B."

Second Grade: "Min is such a loving, charming, funny guy with great ideas and learning capacity—that brain is a sponge! Everyone in the school will miss Min. We have a very special place for him in our hearts. —Mrs. J."

From the librarian: "When Min's walking by or coming in for a book, I hear his aide telling him to try hard not to touch the computers (he loves those keys). He's truly been a bright spot in our day. Full of innocence, highly inquisitive, an endless ball of energy! One of the cutest little loves in the school! —Mrs. S."

Notebooks, we close you now. We purchased a new one for Min's Kentucky school with dancing M&Ms on front. Problem? He's afraid of eyes and wants NOTHING to do with it. I've drawn sunglasses on the M&Ms. He now approves!

Sad goodbyes, but anticipating new hellos,
Brian & Sarah Hampshire

| 11 |

Another Day of Infamy

"... he grew and grew strong as a boy must grow
who does not know he is learning any lessons,
and who has nothing in the world to think of
except things to eat." —Rudyard Kipling [26]

We arrived at our new home with no repercussions. Mom and Dad were right. All my cars fit! My bedroom was tiny, but I had room downstairs for toys. My parents said I would get a bigger room when we do construction. Then my toys could sleep with me.

There was a going-back-to-school picnic with lots of good food. They handed out school supplies—even pencils! I loved them! We sat at a table at the edge of a pavilion because we were brand new.

A random guy asked, "Are you the family from New York?"

We said, "Yes."

He sat across the table from us and said who he was. When I heard his name, I thought it was "Family;" so right from the start I called him "Mr. Family." He laughed and said he loved that. Then he talked-talked-talked. I could tell he loved talking because I did too. I liked him immediately. He would be my special ed teacher and would become my friend.

Then the principal introduced herself and welcomed us, and two teachers said I would be in their combined second- and third-grade class.

I stood up and stomped my foot. "I already finished second grade. I'm not doing that again!"

Dad tried calming me. "It'll give you time to get used to a new school."

I still wasn't happy, but I just met a whole bunch of nice people. *I'm going to like them. Maybe this school will be okay.*

I met my aide who was a Christian. She was hired especially for me and was my aide for as long as I needed one. We became wonderful friends.

Our house needed repairs, but my parents were good at that. My little bedroom ceiling wasn't good though. It had dried leak stains.

One night I walked into my little room to go to bed. Instead, I quick ran downstairs and told my parents, "My ceiling is on my bed."

"Get back to bed," Mom said.

"But the ceiling's on my bed!"

"That's a pretty clever excuse. I'm going up there! If the ceiling's not on your bed, you're in trouble!" Mom marched upstairs.

I followed, and was she ever surprised!

My parents set me up a temporary sleeping area in a downstairs room, where I stayed a good long time.

It was still August when Michael came back from Army training. I was happy he was home from camp and staying until college in January. So was Nathan. My same-brothers were goofballs together. They laughed and fooled-around-fought because that's what they did.

We visited lots of churches then went to one, and I liked it before we even entered because on a hill next to it were three crosses. It sparked emotions and reminded me about Jesus dying for me, and I had

Him in my heart. I was excited to see some friends from school inside. Our family voted, and it was unanimous. This was the church for us!

The special ed bus picked me up for school Tuesday, September 11th like every other day. My same-brothers took Dad to the airport to fly near New York City because Grandma was in the hospital. Mom dropped Stephen at school then met with missionary friends.

I was in class being myself when all of a sudden there was news of catastrophic events in New York, Washington D.C., and a plane that crashed in Pennsylvania. The students were terrified!

I remember seeing what happened on a screen. The towers collapsing reminded me of sand running through an egg timer and ending flat on the bottom—like nothing's left.

I couldn't connect with what happened, but some students had shocked looks on their faces. Some were crying. I jumped out of my chair, and my aide didn't stop me. I hurried to hug the closest kid crying and give comfort. Then I hugged more kids.

Later at Ground Zero, President Bush stood on rubble and said, "... the people who knocked these buildings down will hear all of us soon ..." Then people chanted "USA! USA! USA!" [27]

My eight-year-old self didn't know what that meant, but my adult self knew the President told the enemy to "watch their backs." In our household this meant Michael was going to war. Nathan wanted to go, so he joined the Army.

Now I had two brothers who would go to war. I wanted to go too.

Dear Smith Family Reunion,   *August 2001-January 2002*

Our apologies for the uninvited guest at your event. We didn't know Min used his newfound freedom this way. We learned about it at our son's initial special education meeting when the principal announced, "I hear Min attended the Smith family reunion. He apparently had a wonderful time."

Our jaws hit the floor.

We also learned Min visited one of your kinfolk's home numerous times, declaring he needed food because "my parents don't feed me." Could someone please lift a rock and let us crawl under?

Min loves traipsing up and down our holler. Since it has three little connected roads leading nowhere in particular, we let Min "go" as long as he stays within these. He loves this freedom he'd not enjoyed on our busy road in New York.

We found a friendly church down the road, across the creek. They've taken us in as family, and our new start in Kentucky has been healing.

As Min grew in the Lord, he learned believers have spiritual gifts. He thought, because of his disability, he had none. We reminded him soul and spirit cannot be disabled, and God works through those. We encouraged Min to pray, which seemed to be his spiritual gift. Over time he asked, "Does someone else need prayer?"

God answered Min's prayers for big and small things. For example, Min wanted to see the Northern Lights. We told him they were too far away.

"Can I ask God to let me see them?"

"You can ask Him anything."

Min prayed. To our surprise, a news broadcast announced a solar storm pushed the Northern Lights south, making them visible in our corner of Kentucky! (A sweet friend, touched by this, sent Min a Northern Lights book which he treasures.)

With the arrival of colder weather, Min stayed closer to home.

For Christmas 2001 our daughter and husband came with their two kids. We hadn't met the younger before. What joy—loving on them! Their Uncle Min wasn't sure about them but did enjoy playing with their toys.

But not all felt joyous. The new year found us driving treacherous, icy mountain roads to deliver Michael to his Army unit. They were deployed soon after. Then Nathan left for boot camp. Min wonders if all camps require boots.

Smith family, we're running low on sons. But beware! Min's still in our midst! Once snow leaves the mountains, he'll likely head your way. If he says he's hungry, maybe it's because he hibernated.

Sincerely,

Brian—your neighbor down the holler

| 12 |

Passing On

"God gave us all the gift of life. And the secret and
purpose of life is to return to God ... a beautiful life!"
—*Robert O'Rourke* [28]

Our new town was a heavenly, peaceful place. No one ridiculed or judged us.

Our holler went steep uphill to a dead end. When it snowed and iced, we left our car at the bottom and pulled our way home by hanging onto stuff at the side of the road. When it rained hard, our holler turned into a river. Stephen and me jumped in the water and got all soppy. It was fun. So was the creek in our backyard. I played in it with my rubber snakes.

I liked books about snakes. I checked one out at the library because I now had my own library card. I took out whatever I wanted! This was a big deal and responsibility because, if I lost the library's property, I must pay a fine.

Dad, Mom, and Stephen worked on a new room for me. Dad made me a loft bed with a ladder. I had a little office under it, but I was a messy housekeeper and sometimes lost the library's property.

I went to the library and franticly apologized for returning items late. The librarians spoiled me rotten. They never fined me and even gave me books.

The library had lots of animal books. I checked out the same ones over and over. Mom said I couldn't always get those because others needed a turn. Then someone took out my favorite ones, and I was like Smeagol [29]—I wanted "my precious" books!

I loved the computers there but not the time limit. The librarians gave me extra time anyway, so I was spoiled rotten again. A lot of us kids were. We liked it that way.

Another place I was spoiled was church. When a kid had a birthday, that kid got to grab a handful of coins from a huge jar. Like magic! More money appeared for the next birthday!

When my birthday came, I put my grimy hand in the jar and pulled out a handful of coins. This man said, "Grab another handful," so I did and put it all in my pockets.

I went back to our pew and pulled it all out to show Mom and Dad. The coins went everywhere and made a racket. My parents said to put some in the offering. I stomped my foot. *What's the point of getting money and putting it back? Unfair!*

God wanted me to be a cheerful giver like the widow Jesus taught about—who gave her only coin. She could've done anything with it, but she did the right thing. I needed to give from my heart.

Thurman, the man who let me take the extra handful, helped us a lot. He and his buddy and the sheriff hunted and killed a deer. Then Thurman got it butchered and brought the meat in boxes, and I helped bag it for the freezer.

I loved this tender, delicious meat—especially when Dad grilled it. When we ran out, Thurman brought more.

We had money troubles, and we prayed for food. The meat was part of God's answer. Then God did more.

We were sitting in church, and our preacher-who-loves-Groundhog-Day announced for my parents to come up. He said, "We're giving you a pounding!" (v)

Did we do something wrong? Things seemed to be going perfectly with no repercussions.

My parents went forward cautiously.

Then the preacher-who-loves-Groundhog-Day said the church was giving us bunches of food. My parents were relieved and thankful for this answer to our prayers. A wonderful surprise! After church, they loaded Thurman's pick-up truck to the brim. So, we weren't in trouble. We were blessed.

Another way I was spoiled was when I got blood drawn. It was an absolute horror! Dad held me on his lap and wrapped his arms and legs around me. Mom held my arm straight. Two nurses tried to draw blood. I was being held against my will—like a straight-jacketed prisoner, but I had to have it done. I cried and yelled!

The nurses said, "If you cooperate, we'll buy you ice cream."

I pictured a popsicle, and that motivated me to get this done. When it ended, the nurses collected their money and gave me $5.00! I thanked them profusely. Dad said that was enough to buy a whole box of ice cream.

We went to the store. I wanted chocolate chip cookie dough ice cream. They didn't have that. So, we bought a roll of chocolate chip cookie dough, made little balls, and stuck those in vanilla ice cream. It was Michael's favorite, and he was gone to war. I wanted to share, but my parents said I could keep it. I ate it right out of the box.

What I learned from grown-ups in Kentucky is they cared a lot, and children were important to them. I was spoiltly loved, and it felt good. They sacrificed to help us often. They taught me to give back and be compassionate.

A boy in school was diagnosed with cancer. He got so sick he couldn't come anymore. The school collected money for him and his family. They prayed he would get well, but he passed away.

I wasn't a person who showed many emotions, but I was sad. I didn't think a kid should die of cancer, but the people's prayers were answered because he got well the very minute he went to Heaven.

My mother's sister visited from far, far away. Aunt Carolyn brought me rocks—small ones that fit in my hand. I was delighted. This began a new adventure for me collecting rocks.

One time we went to the Kentucky Reptile Zoo (w) and stopped at a tourist store. They had a bin of unique stones in a multitude of colors. I put some into a small pouch and bought them. They were very special.

Aside from liking these stones, I liked normal ones of a specific shape and size. I found them walking around our holler. Some were in people's driveways, but I asked before taking those. They always said, "Yes."

I randomly carried them in my pockets. When I reached in and felt them, smooth ones calmed me, rough ones made me nervous because I forgot what they were, some felt sandy, and sharp ones made me go "ouch!" But I still loved carrying them, even though my pants slid down from their weight.

My parents bought me a belt. That helped.

I went out of the house with my pockets full of rocks and visited our neighbor. She was sitting on her porch reading a book. I showed her my collection and told her all about them. The neighbor seemed amazed and spent time with me.

Then she had a death in her family. I felt sympathy for her but didn't know how to help until I thought my rocks could be a parting gift. I picked a special one, put it in her mailbox by the road, and went home.

When the neighbor got her mail and saw the rock, she knew who put it there. (She still has that rock.)

I wanted to know more about rocks. I asked my parents, but I also asked random questions about everything because I'm curious and clever.

Mom and Dad's new rule: "Min may only ask one hundred questions each day." *Unfair!*

Dear Scotland   *Spring 2002*

One morning I felt quite nauseous but needed to get our laddies off to school.

Min learned Brian or I must open our bedroom door before going downstairs. Sometimes he played quietly in his room. But generally, he was so full of questions, he wormed his way into the hall and parked outside our door.

This particular morning, I gulped down pink tummy stuff then opened our door.

There sat Min. "In what country do they eat sheep's stomach?"

My eyes widened. I reeled around and tore to the bathroom to "un-eat."

In connection to your country, Min asks about haggis, as you've read. He also asks about the Loch Ness monster, which he learned about from Scooby-Doo!

Enjoy your dinner!

                    —Friends across the "pond"

FYI:

(v) Centuries-old church custom of giving food offerings—"a pound of this—a pound of that"

(w) Slade, Kentucky

| 13 |

Ups and Downs

"I'm a very rare sort of bear," he replied importantly ...
"I emigrated, you know." (Paddington) —Michael Bond [30]

I wanted to go to camp, like my brothers. Stephen worked summers at one, and I knew Nathan and Michael went to Army camp. There were camps nearby, but they didn't accept special needs kids. I was a kid without a camp.

Mom and Dad planned to travel north to places they called "old stompin' grounds" and visit churches that missionary-supported us. There was going to be Camp Dove for special needs kids at the place where my parents met each other.

The camp director accepted me and said they would do sensory integration things to help me. My parents didn't understand that, but they trusted the director because they knew her many years.

I enjoyed being with other kids and with another lady my parents worked with in "good old days." When camp was over, I wanted to go again. But Camp Dove closed.

During another trip to New York, while Mom went to writers' conference, I went to Camp Hope where my parents worked long ago. Dad preached in New York City during the day, and at night Dad and me had it special because we stayed in the staff cabin. I liked that week.

I started going to some random children's hospital. It was wow! They had lots of things on the walls I could press and turn. I loved that. Neurofibromatosis clinic was in the Genetics Department.

The doctors and staff were very nice and wanted to help me. I had x-rays on my spine and legs and blood taken because that's what NF1 kids need done. I would go back next year.

I liked going to the post office and using the special key to open our box. I no longer said "boo" into mailboxes, but I was curious about the wanted posters on the bulletin board. I learned those people did crimes.

One day I went with Mom to the post office and stopped by the posters. I asked if those were like kids' photos at Walmart. Were those kids criminals? Mom said no. They were kidnapped which meant taken. She explained about dangers of bad people who took kids. I was shocked!

Then Mom handed me the special mailbox key, and I charged in. An elderly lady struggled getting mail out of her box. I rushed to help her but forgot to ask, "Do you need help?" and also to put my arm out.

My parents taught me to put my arm out to make sure I wasn't in other people's space because I used to bump into people and be right in their faces, except I wasn't interrogating them.

So, I didn't mean to, but I knocked the elderly lady down. She landed on her bottom. Mom rushed to help her up and apologized profusely. I was extremely sorry too, and the lady accepted my apology.

Mom took me aside and gave me a lecture. She reminded me I still needed to put my arm out to make sure I wasn't in someone's space and said, "You especially need to be careful of old people because, if they fall, they can break their hips."

For a long time after that, whenever I encountered an old folk, I said, "I won't knock you down and break your hips." And they wondered, and some said, "Thank you. I appreciate that."

Another elderly lady who I didn't want to knock down and break her hips was Mrs. Martha—a retired reading teacher with a heart of gold. She was like flowers blossoming. She told my parents, "God laid on my heart to help Min. May I tutor him as my gift to God?"

My parents were astonished and accepted because they knew I struggled in school, even with extra help.

I worked with Mrs. Martha two afternoons each week. When I arrived, I petted the cat and chatted real loud with her husband because of the TV's high volume. He sat in a wheelchair and had dementia, but he remembered me. I loved his enormous wall map with tannish countries and bluish seas. I pointed to my homeland.

Mrs. Martha, Mom, and me enjoyed homemade snacks at the kitchen table. Then straight to work! Mrs. Martha bought gob loads of teaching supplies and expected me to learn but was strictly patient.

Then this loud commercial played on the TV every time, and I laughed and went off track until it ended. Poor Mrs. Martha had to get me back working. She never got fed up or quit though.

I loved Mrs. Martha's dictionary. I always looked through it and a special reptile book she bought. She mostly taught me spelling and how to use the dictionary to up my skill-meter, and she tried her best to teach me cursive writing.

THAT was absolute torture! My eyes moved different directions! I turned and twisted! Even making an "i" was so hard and lifting the pencil to dot it drove me insane, but Mrs. Martha was the cursive warden, and I was the straight-jacketed prisoner.

Finally, my parents intervened and told Mrs. Martha to stop the cursive writing torture, except they didn't say it that way. We didn't know why I couldn't learn it, but I was relieved when Mrs. Martha let me off on good behavior.

When she finished tutoring me for good, she rewarded me with the special reptile book. (I still have it.)

I was in fourth grade when I turned ten years old. My parents gave me a jeans jacket. I always wanted one because Chuck Norris wore one in *Walker, Texas Ranger.* I loved that show, which started when I was in a Korean hospital crib with the top of my head shaved, doing taekwondo baby moves, and being "very impatient baby." [x] All that interested me then was getting milk and having my diaper changed.

So now I had a jacket like Walker, and it felt good. I never wanted to take it off, even in hot weather.

At school I kept my jeans jacket on constantly. My aide said, "Why don't you hang that up?" and I said, "No thank you." My aide wrote in my M&M notebook that I sometimes hid from my parents. But Mom found it and read about me wearing my jeans jacket all day. She wrote, "Min must take off his jacket at school." This upset me to infinity! I must have that jacket on!

One reason I liked it was because it had lots of pockets to carry my rocks and small toys, and it felt even better with my treasures on board. I could also hide the magnitudinous number of pencils I wanted to take to and from school.

One day when I sat jacketless in class, the teacher taught about how we are all different in our own way. She used me for an example— pointing out that I sat with my legs up and crossed because I came from a different culture. I always did that, but now I was embarrassed. I unfolded my legs and put them down, but that sparked me thinking about where and who I came from.

When I got home, I asked Mom, "Who did I come out of?"

She was a little surprised but answered. "Your birth mother."

"Mrs. Choi?"

"No, she was your foster mother." Mom explained the difference.

"Who did my brothers come out of?"

"Me."

I was discombobulated. "I'm the only one that came out of someone else?"

"Yes."

This ended my first curiosity about how I came into being.

Summer came. We learned about a brand-new camp for kids with NF. I had NF, so I was accepted! I could hardly wait! Another camp I could cling to!

The new camp was at the same time as Bible Club Day Camp. Dad needed to drive the bus to transport campers, so Mom drove me there.

We drove super far, filled out many papers, and heard about lots of rules. Then Mom let me go to the boys' cabin and waved goodbye.

I went swimming and was having fun. Later I was moved out of my cabin. *Why am I being moved?* Me and one other camper got a new counselor who was a friendly grandfather-image. I never had a grandpa, so I loved this!

We had more fun the next day when all of a sudden Mom was there. I was shocked! *What's Mom doing here? She's back way early.* Then I saw my suitcases packed.

Mom grabbed my hand and said, "We're outta here!" We got in the car and drove away.

I was silent a while. Then I asked, "Why are you here?"

Mom pulled over and turned around. "Didn't they tell you I was coming?"

I nervously said, "No. Where are we going?"

"Home." Mom cried. "I'm so sorry. They said you had to leave." Mom explained that the director said I didn't fit in with the other campers.

I squinted my eyes and eyebrows. *But I have NF like they do.* I was crushed. I just wanted to be a camper, make friends, and have fun. I had a camp. Now I didn't. I had a substitute grandpa. Now I didn't. This emptied me of hope.

When we got home, Dad was back from Day Camp and came into the kitchen. He hugged me. "Sorry this happened, buddy. Go ahead upstairs." I took my backpack with my paper and pencils and went to my room, but I heard my parents talking.

"I spoke with Min's reassigned counselor," Mom said. "He was livid that the camp sent Min home. He told me he perceived Min and the other camper had additional concerns besides NF, but they were enjoying their 'mini-camp.'"

"Let's just get through Day Camp for now. Maybe the next appointment with the Developmental Disability Department at Min's hospital will give us answers."

Tuesday me and Mom stayed home because Dad said, "Mom's exhausted."

I played in my room and found comfort under my loft bed. My hundreds of trading cards and little cars were there on special shelves Dad made for me. I loved having them close by.

The next morning, we went to Day Camp—like a consolation prize. I turboed down a water slide the counselors made! It was a blast! I didn't mind the grass under my bare feet because I didn't fear bugs yet. I waited in line for another turn, but Mom called me to come. So I did.

Mom said, "Something happened to Dad's eye. We need to pray for him."

It turned out Dad had strokes, and this wasn't a one-time occurrence.

I was supposed to go for special testing after Day Camp, but that didn't happen because Dad was put in a hospital.

When Dad got better, he picked me up at school. At home I saw piles of stuff all over from the under-stairs coat closet. Mom was crouched in there, peeling stuff off the walls.

Stephen said, "Mom's creating Narnia. We'll spread our coats and walk through."

I asked Mom, "What's a Narnia?"

"A magical world, but this is a playhouse for the kids."

By now I had two nephews and one niece. They visited once every-often. We boys moved the piles so Mom could crawl out. Then I helped clean up. I fit better. I was a big help.

I asked, "Can I play in there too?"

"Sure!"

Mom painted and re-interiorated it with multi-colored wallpaper. Dad put in an electric light and built a sink/stove combo. We were ready to move in!

I put the grandkid toys in, and Mom hung our coats on the rod.

Stephen spread the coats apart and said, "Narnia!"

So that's what we called it. I went in, and it felt magical—like my own little world. Like my under-stairs Noah's Ark room felt in New York—safe and protected. It helped me cope—a very big deal because I missed wearing my jeans jacket inside, which hung on a hook in there.

I took my paper and pencils into "Narnia" and made lists using the special booklet Dad made me with all the *Walker, Texas Ranger* episodes. (I still have that.)

Dear Guinness World Book of Records,   *2004 to forever*

This letter is to inquire who owns the most pencils in the world, reason being this is our son's goal. He aspires to be entered in a future publication.

There's a world record for the person who's broken the most pencils across his forehead. This torments Min! He believes pencils should be treated well. He's also concerned how the environmental movement impacts his goal. "If we can't cut down trees to make pencils, that will be apocalyptically awful!" Since 170,000 pencils can be made from an average-sized tree, he'd rest better knowing at least one can be felled.

Min has collected pencils for years. He used to break pencil points under his fingernails—a horrific habit that rattled our nerves. Next, Min used the points to poke holes in his pants. After that, he tore the holes, ruining his clothing. We required him to work and save money to replace the pants. That cured him!

Our son grieved leaving pencils home during school hours. He hid as many as possible in his pockets and sleeves. The school requested Min not bring so many. Thus, we resorted to daily frisking—complete with "hold it, spread 'em," and "assume the position." We patted Min down and confiscated the excess before he boarded his bus.

Min claims he needs five pencils everywhere he goes "in case one breaks." With these he's made thousands of lists in spiral-bound notebooks, memorized the topics, and knows their order. Later, he changed to 8 ½ x 11 white paper, which he uses exclusively. Perhaps his goal should be world record list-holder instead. We'll suggest that.

Please let us know who holds your world record to help our son gauge how many more pencils he must acquire. Thank you.

Sincerely and "to the point,"

No. 2 parents

P.S.—Thinking storms were moving in, we waited to take this letter to the post office. Turns out the "rolling thunder" was Min sharpening all his pencils.

FYI:

[x] From Min's Korean child study notes received in 2021

| 14 |

Operation Protection Overload

"It's possible he is extra adventurous with no sense of danger ..." —Kathy Hoopmann [31]

The next summer I was at a state park pool with my parents and Bible Club Day Camp kids. I went inside the building to use the bathroom without my parents' knowledge.

After I finished, I met this random stranger. He didn't have a kid with him or a bag of swimming stuff. He offered to buy me candy, and I said, "Yes!" I loved candy! Especially Skittles! He took me to the concession stand and bought me some.

He said he had more goodies in the car. I wanted to check it out. It was like a cartoonish smoke finger ushering me to come to him except I didn't float in the air. I went because I wanted Skittles. He still held onto them, and we walked toward the exit where cars parked. He still didn't have a bag with swim clothes. Just Skittles and me.

I heard a female voice scream my name. I turned around, saw Mom, and stopped. She screamed again. "MIN! COME RIGHT NOW!" I thought *I better listen to avoid any more screaming,* so I sped toward her.

Mom shook me and hugged me. "What on earth do you think you're doing?" Her voice trembled.

"He bought me Skittles, but he didn't give me the candy yet." I looked back and pointed toward the man, but he vanished. So did my Skittles.

Mom grabbed my hand and took me to the pool area where Dad was. I had to sit by Mom the rest of the time while she ranted and raved about stranger danger. My mind still didn't tell me I put myself in danger. I was fixated on the candy, but now I didn't get anything except in trouble.

My parents wanted to help me have success. They bought a roll of tickets, and I could earn those toward prizes and even eating out! I kept them in a clear zip-lock bag taped to the refrigerator and watched it fill up. I tried very hard.

Even though I had a bad camp experience the year before, I wanted to try again. My parents wished me to have enjoyment but were afraid to have me out of their peripheral vision. But they found a special needs camp in another part of Kentucky. Then they saw the price. "We can't afford this."

I asked if we could pray. We did, and God gave me a full scholarship. That answer to prayer gave us confidence that Camp KYSOC was okay. I loved the staff people, and some even knew about Jesus as their Savior. This was the camp for me! I couldn't wait to go again the next summer!

That August I redid fourth grade again. I was fuming mad until my parents said I would already know some stuff and be at the head of the class. Then my anger subsided. I had the same teacher again. I figured she was held back too, so we had something in common and good bonding.

My special testing at Developmental Disability Department (DDD) was rescheduled because Dad had strokes the year before. The tests seemed like all games to twelve-year-old me.

When they were done, we sat at a table with the main doctor. I was drawing. The doctor said I had something called Asperger's. She explained it was a form of autism. It wasn't making sense to me, so I kept drawing.

But my parents got quiet. I glanced up and saw relief-sadness on their faces. The doctor talked more about results and ways to help me. She scheduled me to meet with a therapist who would become an important figure in my life and help me cope with Asperger's. This was a big piece of the puzzle to put my life together—a mix of sadness and hope.

Hey Elephant in the room!   *2005*

Do you know that old adage? Well, there's one in our house. You! I look back and think—Idiot, wasn't it obvious? Min's Asperger form of autism. (We'd thought NF1 was the beast, but ...)

From May 1996 until one not-so-fine 2005 day, we maneuvered around you. Then a doctor who "trained pachyderm" said, "You have an elephant in the room." (She didn't actually, but that's what we heard.) We gleaned hints prior but still blinked in disbelief, yet there you were—plain as day.

Now, Elephant, hold on. This is about to get gross from your perspective.

When I'm overwhelmed, blurting our world's coming to an end, Brian says, "How do you eat an elephant?" I reply, "One bite at a time," because that's what oh-wise-one taught me. Free therapy! Cheaper than psychiatry! It breaks down difficulties into "bite-sized" solutions, constantly needed with Min.

By now you're ready to stomp the livin' daylights out of us. Please refrain! After all, we've given you room and board for nearly a decade.

Here's what we learned: We must remember this is an elephant, house it appropriately, give it a proper diet, and train it. Hard? At times, seemingly impossible. When it overwhelms, we must deal with it "one bite at a time." But, knowing it's an elephant helps.

So, make yourself at home, and we'll try to remain hospitable.

> *Letting you live,*
> *your "keepers"*

My DDD therapist showed my parents ways to help me and told them about a book that explained Asperger's very well—*The Out-of-Sync Child.*[32]

I saw Mom reading that. "What's an out-of-sync child?"

"A kid like you." Then Mom explained more about sensory deprivation.

Yep, that sounded like me, and we began to understand me better.

Mom and Dad bought a platform swing. Dad took down my double closet doors and hung it in the opening. I could swing and spin as often as I needed. They helped me understand time with a special timer. [y] As minutes passed, the red disappeared and turned white, so I knew how much time remained which helped at home and school.

Then one day a light went on over Mom's head, but not really because there wasn't one there. She said, "I know now why Min always wants to wear his jeans jacket—the weight of it, like when he used to wear the weighted vest years ago. It comforts him."

Yes, it did, and it also helped me feel arms. I already had arms, but having them covered in thick cloth comforted me.

FYI:

[y] Southpaw Enterprises, Dayton OH

| 15 |

Major Upsets

"God knows what's good, what's right, and what's best ..."
—*Elizabeth Elaine Watson* [33]

What's going on with me? I had headaches. I took naps, and they went away. There was a really bad one. I held my head with both hands as hard as I could, but it didn't help. I looked super bad the next morning. Mom said, "You're staying home." She gave me headache pills, and I slept a lot. Then I felt better.

Now I didn't want to sleep in my loft bed. I was afraid of climbing and the height, so I started sleeping underneath. Dad shortened the legs, then I was okay for a while. I wouldn't go on my big spinning swing anymore—opposite of when I spinned forever.

Our town had a festival every year, and we heard the fun from our house. I asked if Stephen could take me to the big rides, and my parents said yes, because no matter where I went with Stephen, he always brought me back.

We walked there and bought tickets. I was over-the-roof excited about the marvelous designs of the attractions! There was a Ferris wheel with swinging cages. Stephen really got ours going. I scrunched in a fetal position and begged him to stop. He did, and we finished the ride.

Next, we went to another ride. Stephen didn't go on, but I did. It just started, but I couldn't stand it. Stephen noticed I looked freaked and asked the man to stop it. I was tipsy getting off.

I took some deep breaths, and we bought soda. Then we walked to the other end of the festival and met up with our parents.

Mom took one look at me and exclaimed, "What in the world happened?"

Stephen explained.

Mom and Dad didn't know what was going on. Neither did I, but something changed in me.

2006 I became a teenager—a big deal because I was growing up. Mom and Dad made me a weighted lap pad and weighted blanket. It felt like how I wished my birth mother might've embraced me or maybe like I was in a womb. A secure, safe barrier.

I loved our Kentucky town. It was paradise, and no one wronged us. I had five good years in New York and now almost five in Kentucky. This was home to us now.

Then a phone call changed everything—a family emergency. We must sell our house and go. I wasn't a fan of things I didn't know or understand. This gripped me fearfully.

Then more bad news in my perspective. Stephen graduated and joined the Army. Now all three brothers would have boots, but the war continued. I worried for Stephen's safety. He already was my brother for ten years, but he was also my close friend.

It was the end of an era. I got through fifth grade without my aide over my shoulder all the time. A very big deal! And in the lunchroom, I coped because the staff was kind, and friends like Blake helped me. She shared her Doritos too.

I was happy on the outside but sad inside. Soon I needed to say goodbye. I would miss everyone and the lunchroom ladies because I loved people who handed out food! My school made me a heartwarming book full of letters, saying what I meant to them—a very special treasure. (I still have this memorabilia.)

At the end of Bible Club Day Camp, we would move. I was supposed to help pack while my parents took turns there. *If I don't pack, I won't have to go.* That idea failed because the counselors packed my stuff.

Then they loaded the moving truck for us! My parents were spent, so they were thankful to infinity.

Time to go. I went up the holler to say goodbye to friends and forgot to come back for a while. When I got home, Mom wasn't happy, but then we had another problem.

The cat vanished. We looked everywhere, we psss-psss-psssed, but no cat. *Uh oh. Kitty's in trouble.* We went out to eat. I liked that part of moving. When we came back, the cat was waiting. We were minus the cat two hours.

Dad led the way with the moving truck. I was in the back seat of the car on pet duty. I liked that part of moving. Mom drove, and Stephen was navigator. When we got down a major highway, traffic stopped. Dad walkie-talkied Mom and told her there was a massive accident, and they were detouring everyone.

Mom walkie-talkied back. "Did you notice our travel time?"

Dad replied, "Two hours."

We realized God had the cat disappear—not like vanish in thin air—but go off somewhere, and that's why we left late. Now in-trouble cat was Super-Kitty!

Kaleidoscope,   *February through August 2006*

You're a toy Min enjoys. You hold broken pieces of this-n-that in one end, which turns. Looking through the other end and turning you, though, creates one beautiful design after another.

We're broken. An emergency compels us to leave southeastern Kentucky—something we never thought we'd do. We'll be near our daughter and her kids.

Kaleidoscope, even amidst broken pieces, we know God does all for the good [z] *and will create something beautiful in His perfect time. With this in mind, we begin anew—again.*

Clinging to Hope,
willing servants

FYI:
[z] Referencing Romans 8:28-29

| 16 |

Winds of Change

"… Tis true my form is something odd—But blaming me is blaming God …" —Isaac Watts [34]

We went from a mountain holler in a small quaint town to a huge military city. At our new home, we heard cannons, mortar fire, and helicopters. I thought we were being attacked, but the Army played war to prepare for war. After I realized that, when helicopters flew over, we ran outside and yelled super loud, "THANK YOU!"

We went to this location to be near my niece and nephews. Sometimes I wanted to play with them and sometimes I didn't, but we all enjoyed the trampoline. My niece remembered I used to sit "criss-cross applesauce" while they jumped. I'd lift in the air like I was sitting and land in the same position. It made them giggle immensely.

Mostly I didn't get along with my niece. She pouted and had tantrums. I didn't like her noise, but her kicking on the floor looked funny. One time, though, I went up to my niece and gave her a bear hug. She was so surprised because I never hugged her before.

We had a little pool in our yard. One nephew was terrified of water. Dad held him, gently rubbed water on him, and lowered him tiny bits. My parents learned this worked because they tried it with three-year-old me. This nephew became a little guppy like me. He was a little tike, but we played together. He was my kind of people.

My other nephew liked the same things as me, even though he was six years younger, but he mostly played alone. When it was time to go home, he wanted to stay—so did the others. My niece cried, and it was contagious because her brothers cried too. I stayed away and didn't catch it.

In summers I still went to Camp KYSOC and made crafts, ate food, rode on a boat, and fished. So many fun things! One of my favorites was stringing beads in the arts and crafts building. I also went on bead hunts and collected ones scattered around the cabins. I put them in my KYSOC carry-bag to bring home and make necklaces during the year. (I still love stringing beads.)

That fall Stephen graduated from Army training in Missouri. Dad needed to help at a wedding in New York, so Mom and me drove many hours to the Army ceremony. Nathan came too because he was home from deployment.

As we drove along, Mom asked me to search radio stations for news.

I pushed all the buttons, which I always enjoyed doing, and surprise! This lady named Aretha sang her famous spelling song.[aa] "That's the lady who sings L-A-R-S-P-E-D!"

Mom laughed. "Yup, that's what we all need—a little more 'lar-sped!'"

I agreed.

I really liked going to Missouri. It felt like our Kentucky home because there were hills, and they had interesting rocks.

I was happy Stephen finished training and was coming home! But his unit was relocated immediately. The soldiers got on the bus, and we waved goodbye. Then it sunk in. Stephen wasn't coming home.

Here I was, the only kid left in the household. I dearly missed my brothers. I coped by playing computer war games (that were theirs) and imagined fighting battles together because I couldn't go. The Army wouldn't take me.

Mom said I could be a civilian and help soldiers and their families. That sounded good to me.

My school was its own war zone with security built into the walls. An officer patrolled the front. The cafeteria was filled with people, but I felt alone. My classroom was in its own wing for disabled kids to make us feel like we belonged, but in our wing some students called me "big head." I did have a big head, but they weren't stating fact. I hated that to infinity and felt miserable.

Another annoying thing? I got picked to represent my class in the all-school spelling bee. My parents were excited and proud I was chosen, but I desperately wanted out of it! Seems Mrs. Martha's help paid off because here I was S-T-U-C-K!

The spelling bee took place in the auditorium. To get there I passed a pencil vending machine. For $.25 I could buy a pencil any time. I carried a bunch of quarters because pencils fascinated me. I had to have them!

Spelling bee time! I stood on stage with the others, and there were more than one-thousand eyes looking at me if everyone had two of them, which I'm pretty sure they did. I wasn't ommetaphobic anymore, but those eyes belonged to living beings. First word: Correct! Second word: Wrong! I was mad at first then relieved to be done.

Another thing I did well was chess. My parents asked if I could join that club. The teacher in charge welcomed me. I used to watch my brothers play. I don't know how I got good at it, but the teacher said, "Min has a natural inclination."

This location is where I learned to ride a two-wheel bike. Now I transported myself around the neighborhood. I was born to be a wild biker-dude. In fact, my bike's design was like a motorcycle.

My jeans jacket didn't fit anymore. I wanted to be like Dad, so I asked, "Could I please have a leather jacket for my birthday?"

My parents snickered. "Hmm. They cost a lot, and you'd have to take good care of it." But my parents already got a deal on one. They were sneaky that way.

I was pretty responsible with my leather jacket because I knew the dog liked beef, and maybe she'd eat it since it was formerly a cow. I loved this jacket! It was even heavier than my jeans one, it made me feel grown up, and I looked like Dad.

One day I put on my leather jacket, got my bike out, and hit the road. After a while, I rode home, put my bike in the shed, and locked the door.

When we returned from a trip, someone had broken in and stole my bike. I was angry! I wanted justice! The police said there was almost zero chance my bike would be found. I was heartbroken.

My mode of transportation! Gone! I was grounded but not punished-grounded. Mostly I stayed home and resorted to indoor activities until Dad and Mom discovered Buddy Ball—Special Needs Athletic League.

We did basketball, bowling, and softball. At basketball I waddled like a penguin with hands in my pockets. My parents yelled, "Get your hands out, and catch the ball!" So I did. Then bowling. I came in top bowler and was safe to bowl with because I didn't throw the ball in the air anymore. Then softball. Once I slid into fourth base. Everyone cheered, but I got tagged. At the Buddy Ball banquet, we got trophies. (I'm still proud of mine.)

In the summer we lived on less money because some people who helped with missionary support couldn't give then. One Sunday morning my parents asked me to pray with them for God to supply our needs, so we prayed.

Later someone knocked on our door. I peeked around the corner. Three young fellows from Estonia were selling books for the summer, needed a place to stay, and would pay rent. Dad told Mom, "This is God's answer." He arranged it with the fellows.

We emptied our living room, borrowed beds, and made them a place to call home. They didn't sell books in the evenings, so it was like having temporary brothers.

Before the next summer came, we planned to move again. I was glad this time because I didn't like it except for Buddy Ball, and the next place was closer to camp.

I was driven to and from school every day for two years. The last day Mom ran late, and "riders" were already out. "Walkers" were released, so I went with the flow. *I don't see Mom. Then it's okay to walk home.* I crossed the busy road by the crossing guard and continued the mile-and-a-half home.

When I reached our yard, Mom pulled in the driveway. She got out and slammed the car door. "I've looked all over for you! You scared me to death!"

"I didn't see you, so I walked home."

We headed into the house, and Dad heard the racket. Mom told him what happened, and I had to sit through the scolding.

"We've picked you up every day for two years, and you think it's okay to walk? What were you thinking!" Dad exclaimed.

"That it was okay because Mom wasn't there."

I was sorry I scared my parents again, like three years prior with the stranger-danger incident. My Mom ended up sorry she ran late, but neither parent understood why I did it. But deep down inside I was proud I made it home all by myself!

Dear Military Presence,   *2006-2008*

Min thanks you everywhere we go and proudly tells you he's a civilian. He doesn't understand this "rank" comes with no uniform, medals, or stripes.

Some weekends our grandkids visit—a plus for Min to see them and try to interact.

One day our young granddaughter asked, "Who will take care of Uncle Min when you die?"

I was taken aback. "He'll be okay. Why?"

"He will need someone to take care of him," she said then scooted off to play.

What a curious perception from a seven-year-old!

We took Min to a hospital for his annual NF1 checkup where doctors believed he had an additional genetic concern. They tested for Fragile X (a genetic retardation). Result: Negative. They never solved this puzzle.

Military presence, we're not as tough as you. Roger that? Realizing our son's dealing with another issue bent our hearts. In addition, ministry hadn't taken root, the situation with our daughter deteriorated again, and we barely saw our grandkids.

They were permitted one last visit. During that weekend, two police officers came to our door, relaying they received a distress call concerning children at our home.

Terror gripped me! I left them at the door and called the kids, asking if they pranked on the phone. They looked shocked and said "no." I went back and told the police there'd been no problem, I didn't know why they received that call, and the children insisted they hadn't placed one. The police left.

Weak-kneed, I bee-lined to the family room where Brian hadn't heard what happened. Did our daughter place the call or the man she went to twelve years earlier—the one Min called "the bad man?" We knew they maintained contact.

The next day we phoned the police to learn who called them. They wouldn't reveal more—only that it came from outside our area code, still pointing to the same suspects.

Our New York file from 1997 was due to be sealed if no other claims were brought against us. We sought God, and—after only two years here—made plans to go. Again.

Then another scare with Min making an error in judgment—the walking-home-from-school incident! He was fifteen now! Why did he still do these things? Asperger's? Headaches interfering with processing information? NF "kicking up a storm" or the undiagnosed genetic puzzle?"

Min had an MRI before we moved. Results showed a small tumor growing in the midbrain of his brainstem and three tiny lesions. We'd be sure Min's genetics doctor received these results. But for now, we must pack.

Military presence, we're bugging out! Thank you for your service. You'll remain in our prayers.

Over and out—

the civilian's parents

FYI:
(aa) Aretha Franklin singing "Respect" (by Otis Redding)

| 17 |

Twists and Turns

"Jesus ... is happy when you tell Him about your needs,
your joy, your hunger, your pain, your fears ..."
—*Corrie ten Boom* (teacher of special needs children)[35]

We moved to a small, northern Kentucky town close to Camp KYSOC. I still was a camper, but I thought it would benefit me to work there someday—a real possibility and the kind of place I could navigate with people who understood me. And the counselors treated campers the same way God treated people.

I thought I would miss seeing my niece and nephews in our new location, but God did something that seemed sad-happy. They went to live with their father, and it turned out they were near enough for us to visit. They stayed overnight sometimes too. So, even though it was different, it was like "good old days" and a wonderful surprise!

Across the street from our house was this giant siren for tornado warnings. I liked living by the siren. It made me feel safe. I didn't like it because it was loud but only in my left ear.

Not long after we moved in, the siren went off. A storm knocked out power for eleven days. It was a disaster—not the storm—losing electricity because I loved electronics. I coped by using my imagination and designing comic covers for Scooby-Doo. I also sorted my thousands of trading cards over and over.

We drove to the library because their power turned on before ours. It was on the town square, which I didn't know if it was actually a square or a rectangle. Mom and Dad checked e-mail while I browsed and did computer with my library card code.

After this I wanted to go to the library by myself. My parents thought maybe I could because I walked all the way home from school before we moved.

This town was laid out on a grid with streets making right angles—like a maze, and I loved mazes. But I had a problem. I didn't know left from right, even though I was fifteen.

So, my parents taught me to put my pointer fingers straight up and make right-angles with my thumbs. This made a frontwards and backwards "L." Then they asked which one was the correct "L," and I showed them, and they said that was left, so the other one was right. That's how I learned. (I still need to do that.)

We bought a blue and red bike with gears at the Goodwill Store —way different from my stolen bike. I used to stop with my feet on the pedals. This one stopped with hands on the handlebars. For a while, I ran into stuff.

Dad decided I needed a phone. That gave me responsibility and more freedom. Since I wanted to go to the library and neighborhood store by myself, my parents tested me. It took a while, but finally I gave correct directions, so my parents knew I was ready. This was a magnitudinous deal!

I entered this middle school as an eighth grader. At first, I was teased. The head-size thing again. I hated that, but I didn't react as much because I was used to this from our last location. I went to regular classes for a little while, but it wasn't working.

We decided to put me downstairs in the special ed class. I liked it there and was happy. Then kids who teased me stopped because they wondered where I went. My parents felt like they failed by putting me in the special ed room, but I made friends in my new environment.

Dear Mrs. Beethoven, [bb]   *Autumn of 2008*

Why am I writing to you? Because I'm amazed how your son, Ludwig, overcame discordant beginnings, transforming his gift into a symphony. [36] *So did our son.*

I was sorting photos and other memorabilia when Min mentioned Ludwig.

He joined me and pointed to a photo. "Who are they?"

"My parents."

"Are they dead?" he asked as he always does about everyone.

"Yes," I answered.

"Would they like me?"

"Not like. Love." I continued thumbing through the pile.

"How do you know?"

"Because of this." I showed Min a photo of a little boy on a card with Korean and English writing. "When your Aunt Carolyn and I were little girls, our family sponsored a Korean orphan.

"Is he dead?"

"I don't know. An uncle adopted him, then we lost touch."

Min picked up an old "World Vision Magazine" with the Korean Orphan Choir [37] *on front. "They're wearing hanboks, and they look like me! I wonder if any are my family."* [cc]

"They toured here, and we went to hear them sing." I recalled a YouTube video of them singing on an Art Linkletter program. [38] *"Wanna hear them?"*

"Yeah." Min listened intently, his eyes glued on the orphans.

"On one of their tours, a deaf girl sang in sign language."

"Deaf like Beethoven!" he exclaimed.

"Hmm. I hadn't thought of that, but yeah."

At the end, Art Linkletter explained the children were orphaned, like he was.

"He was an orphan too?" Min asked.

"Apparently."

"Is he dead?"

This is how most discussions go.

One day Min came home from middle school and asked, "What's a retard?"

I went wide-eyed. "A not-very-nice way of saying someone's mentally disabled. Did someone call you that?"

"Maybe," he said quietly. "Am I a retard?"

I hesitated. "Retarded, yes."

Min looked horrified. "That's not very nice!"

"You asked, and we always said we'd be honest, even about hard stuff. The noun 'retard' isn't nice, but the verb 'retard' or 'retarded' shares another definition."

Our son adores dictionaries. He'll read one over a story any day, so mentioning "definition" caught his attention.

I thumbed through our music books, pulled out a concerto, and sat next to Min—opening it midway and pointing to a word. "Read that."

"I can't read cursive. Is it okay to say cursive since it has 'curse' in it?"

"You're changing the subject, and it's not cursive. Just fancy-like." I tapped my finger near the word. "So read it."

"Retard." He bobbed his head in surprise.

"It's a musical term. When you asked if you're retarded and I said yes, that just means you think slower."

"Because of NF?"

"That or the other genetic puzzle. In music, though, 'retard' is part of the masterpiece."

"Oh. Can I get a snack?"

"Sure."

Why tell you this, Mrs. Beethoven? Because our sons share something in common. Their giftedness? Perhaps. For your son? Music, of course. Despite Ludwig's disability, he continued his life's work—composing.

Min hears background music and knows in what production it belongs (some composed by your son)—probably due to Asperger's. Min's true giftedness, however, comes from his heart!

First his rocks. Nothing special about most of them, but, when a neighbor lost a loved one, Min expressed his sympathy by placing a favorite rock in her mailbox. Later she shared, "That was the sweetest thing a child ever did for me, and it filled me with happiness and love for Min." And other neighbors who experienced loss found rocks in their mailboxes too.

Then this: When visitors were leaving, we urged Min to take part in saying goodbye. Once, though, when his nephews and niece were heading home, Min came without prompting and lifted his niece in a tight embrace.

Our granddaughter's face beamed, and she squealed with delight. "Uncle Min hugged me! He never hugged me before!"

And then Min's prayers. He doesn't articulate beautifully, but God honors his simple words, answering more times than we can count. Our son recognizes this and comments, "God must really love me."

Mrs. Beethoven, your son continues to be revered worldwide.

Min will leave his mark too—remembered by all who received a rock, a hug, or an answer to his prayers.

You see, the music of Min's heart are his masterpieces. The little rocks? His "Moonlight Sonata." That first hug? His "Für Elise." Those simple prayers? His "Ode to Joy." [39]

What pride we mothers share as we ponder our sons' gifts!
With a symphony in my heart,
one recognizing purpose in her discordant note

FYI:
(bb) Ludwig van Beethoven's mother
(cc) Due to appearance and dress

| 18 |

When Life Turns on Its Head

"Does anyone know what it is like to lose two mothers
in a lifetime?" (Ava Rose) —Cleo A. Lampos
(foster child, special education teacher)[40]

At my middle school, an upstairs friend was a super nice boy from China. His family ran a Chinese restaurant in town. I liked playing with his little brother while we waited for take-out. He had little cars but not many. I gave him some of mine.

The father and mother were kind and sometimes gave me extra food. I said thank you—"gamsahamnida"—with a traditional bow. I liked going there for more than the food. It sparked my mind about my Asian roots.

My parents were in the kitchen. I came to them and asked, "Who are my mother and father?"

"Do you remember asking who you came out of?" Mom asked.

"I guess, but I don't remember their names or anything about them."

"Do you really want to know, no matter what? It might be painful to hear," Dad said.

"I'm all right with that."

We kept my memory book on the living room shelf. Mom said to get it, and we sat at the kitchen table.

I opened it and saw photos of me as a toddler and some as a baby. I could look at it whenever I wanted, but now I needed to connect. My parents recorded my Korean history in red ink and my American in blue ink. My birth parents' names were in red.

"Your birth mother and birth father ..." Mom started to say.

"Mrs. Choi and her husband?"

"No. They were your foster parents. They came later. Your birth parents worked at a factory and lived together."

"What! They weren't married? They committed adultery to have me?" That set me in anger and a depressed state. I didn't like it, but Dad warned this might be hard to hear. "Then I'm a sin! A bastard!"

Mom looked shocked. "How do you even know that word?"

"From school." My head hung down.

"You're not a sin," Dad said, "but you did come to be born this way. You, though, were a miracle because every baby is."

"Your birth father left when he learned your birth mother was pregnant," Mom explained.

I erupted like a volcano! "Who does that to their kid! I don't want to talk about this anymore!" I slammed the book closed and got ready to throw it.

Dad stopped me. "That won't help. Just put it away for now."

I took that stupid book, shoved it back on the shelf, and walked away. I went upstairs, threw myself on the bed, buried myself under pillows, and cried.

It would take me a long, long time to absorb this information. Years, in fact.

Because we lived closer now, we returned to the same random children's hospital with the same doctors and therapist. It was sanctuary for me because everything was familiar. I wanted to run over and play with all the fun gizmos on the wall, but now I was older and knew

I needed to be careful. I played with them some, though, then we went to my genetics appointment.

Dad, Mom, and me checked in, and Mom said to the department coordinator, "Will you make sure Min's recent MRI results are included? We want to review those with the doctor. That tumor they spotted is quite concerning."

The coordinator said, "Oh, that's just an NF thing. The other hospital wasn't used to looking at NF brains."

My parents breathed relief. When I had my MRI before we moved, they remembered there were also three lesions spotted, so they thought, *this is what she's talking about.* We trusted my doctor and people there because we knew them since I was young.

And now they added a nephrologist to my list of doctors because of high blood pressure. NF people needed their kidneys checked.

I got scheduled with a new-to-us family doctor in town for my checkups and regular illnesses. Dr. Mark was a super nice guy. He had experience with autism, so he understood me very well. He looked in my eyes, nose, mouth, and throat then checked my left ear with his otoscope.

"Can you see light coming out the other side?" I smiled.

"You're quite a jokester! No, I can't. That's good news!" Then he checked my right ear. "Whoa! There's something going on in there."

I turned away from Mom, lowered my head, and whispered, "It's a bean."

But Mom overheard. "What!" she cried but not tears. "Why on earth would there be a bean in your ear?"

"I put it there. I found it in the bathroom closet upstairs behind the towels."

Mom looked confused. "There's no closet in that bathroom."

"Not here. When we lived in the mountains."

Mom's jaw dropped. "That's ..." she counted on her fingers, "five years ago! And, besides, why would there be a bean up there?"

I shrugged. "I think a mouse brought it up." In my mind I thought, *so if you're gonna blame anybody, blame the mouse!*

Dr. Mark laughed and rolled his eyes. "Let's flush it out." He had the nurse get the equipment.

Having water jetted into my ear felt unsettling, but I dealt with it because I must face the consequences of my actions. I didn't get punished, though, because Mom said, "Having a bean in there all that time, disrupting your hearing, and needing it flushed out seems punishment enough."

I apologized profusely.

Mom kept shaking her head and saying, "Oh my word! Oh my word! Oh my ..."

The doctor finished flushing it out, and sure enough. In all the goo and guck? A bean.

Suddenly I could hear better. And the next time the siren went off, I covered my ears. It was horrendous!

I was in high school. Ninth grade. All four grades were combined in my special ed classroom, but I went to regular science class. The kids there were really nice and didn't tease me.

Because I had a good year, the school permitted me to go to Colorado because Stephen was being deployed again, but I had to do a report on the trip.

Dad went to see Stephen come back from his first deployment, so now Mom took her turn because my parents tried to go all seven times my brothers were deployed. I was navigator, and this would be a birthday trip. I was turning seventeen soon.

The plan was to stay with our long-time friends, Glenn and Karen, who moved there. When we walked into their house, I asked if I was allowed upstairs since I was older than eight because years ago, I destroyed their son's room. It wasn't funny then. But now everything was swept under the rug, and we had a good laugh.

I went upstairs and found a room with an old man called "Grandpa." Numerous model war planes he made hung from the ceiling. We talked about the planes and war. It very interested me.

Glenn and Karen took Mom, Stephen, and me to Focus on the Family (dd) where Adventures in Odyssey [41] was located. So many fun things to explore! Everything seemed real to me. I loved it and their recorded adventures.

I wrote about my travels and got an excellent grade on my report.

Next, I did a project for science class. I remembered the grandpa's model planes that intrigued me and "Animated Hero Classics" [42]—one about the Wright brothers. They accomplished a great feat. *If they could accomplish what they did, I can too.*

So I picked them. I made a model of their plane out of barbecue skewers, toothpicks, and paper. My parents cut paper for the wings because I can't cut much with scissors, but I did the rest with help holding sticks till the glue dried.

When I brought it to school, everyone was amazed. My science teacher put it on display. I felt like I accomplished something, like the Wright brothers! In a way, I did because I completed one year of high school.

There was an end-of-the-year Western-theme pep rally with some staff dressed in cowboy outfits. The vice-principal pulled a rolling horse while the principal rode on it and "bang-bang-banged" a toy pistol in the air.

Summer came, and I had lots of free time. I listened to *Adventures in Odyssey* and could hear much clearer with the bean out of my ear. It felt better with no vegetable in there. And I imagined the stories in a whole new way.

One of my favorites was "Karen," [43] about a girl with cancer. Even though it spread, she kept her faith and did things happily until she died. I emoted sadness and grief, but it helped me face trials.

Another favorite was "It Is Well" [44] about Horatio Spafford who lost his business in the Chicago fire and most of his family to death. Out of his troubles, he wrote the words to "It Is Well with My Soul." I knew what death was. My friend's great-grandmother died and so did the boy when I was in fourth grade.

When Dad did raceway ministry, Mom drove him so we could use the car. Sometimes Mom said, "Wanna go on an adventure?" I usually said, "Yes." The dog came too. Before we left, my job was to put the cat in the house. I did, then I got into the car.

Mom backed out of the driveway and started down the road. "Oh, by the way, did you let the cat in?"

"Yeah, but I'm not sure it was our cat."

Mom laughed so much. "Let's hope so!"

Mom let me pick which way to turn, like a game. Sometimes we ended up at Dairy Queen by the river, listened to the ambiance of sounds, and ate ice cream. The dog waited patiently because we gave her the bottom of our cones.

I also looked forward to my own adventures at Camp KYSOC. Going to camp was as special as Christmas and my birthday combined. I could hardly wait to see people who were like family to me—Mr. Jim, the counselors, campers—especially "Speedy" who was even faster than me and my friend since my first year.

We shopped for my supplies. I was as excited at age seventeen as at age twelve. Camp was like training for me because I still wanted to work there in the future. I took this very seriously. My dream job!

Then my world collapsed! My favorite camp shut down—like a tornado hit without the warning siren. Everyone connected to camp was distraught and devastated. They tried to raise funds to keep it open. I even gave my $10.00, but it wasn't enough. I was now a teen without a camp and a future adult without my dream job.

Dear Praying Mantis,   *Summer 2010*

Thank you for your brief yet meaningful visit with Min. There you were, traveling through our cracked-cement carport, likely seeking munchables. You froze. Our son came closer. You still didn't move.

Min squatted near you, picked grassy tips growing between the cracks, then laid them on his opened hand.

You tip-toed to him, contemplated the offering, climbed onto his hand, and nibbled. Min didn't freak as usual when a bug landed on him. He remained still, eyes glued on you, silent. When you were done, you hopped off and went your way.

Min often comments, "Remember when the praying mantis climbed on my hand and ate and you didn't think it would and I wasn't scared?"

I've pondered that moment too. Did you sense our son needed your touch? That he was hurting? Was this a God-moment? He surely joys in our delighting.

This may-never-happen-again moment brought our son a smile when you gifted him with your presence. Thank you for leaping by, directed by your Creator, to give joy and make a memory that may last a lifetime.

Sincerely,

one who's not quite as fond of you

FYI:

(dd) Colorado Springs, CO

| 19 |

The Downward Spiraling

"... there are bad times when we cause a lot of hassle
for other people, but what we really want is to be able
to look toward a brighter future."
—*Naoki Higashida* (person with autism)[45]

The next month school started—tenth grade with the same class-mates plus a new kid. I would have another good year.

One day in class a kid took an eraser cap off of a pencil and filled it with hand sanitizer. He dared me to squeeze it.

I took the dare, stuff gushed out, and I overreacted. I threatened, "I'm gonna bring a gun!" I tried to take my words back. "I mean a water gun." The kid snitched on me, and I was sent to the office immediately. I lowered my head and didn't make eye contact with anyone.

The principal called in my parents who arrived not knowing what happened. They were embarrassed and angry with me for doing some-thing so stupid. Then the principal said for one week my parents must bring me into the office, I had to be searched thoroughly, then some-one must be with me the whole school day—even in the bathroom.

Dad and Mom were upset with this decision, but I had to pay the consequences because students signed to obey school rules each year.

We talked more at home.

"I don't know why I got into serious trouble because the principal had a gun in school."

"What're you talking about?" asked Dad.

"At the pep rally last spring they dressed in Western theme. The principal waved a pistol in the air shooting it, so I didn't think saying something about a gun was a problem."

Mom and Dad looked at each other and shook their heads.

Then Dad said, "The no-tolerance policy is harsh and over-the-top in this case, but we'll have to deal with it."

I went through that week of punishment and humiliation and was glad to be free when it ended. I didn't want to get in trouble again and be grounded because a special event was coming soon.

A Camp KYSOC reunion, and we went! Leaves were falling, so it looked different than summer. I walked all over enjoying activities. Mr. Jim described nature things. There was a bug race and hay ride wagon pulled by a tractor. Lots of people came. We didn't raise enough money to reopen camp, but we treasured this very nice goodbye.

Dad took a missionary trip to South America. He left way before Thanksgiving and wouldn't be back till almost Christmas.

On December 7th at school, we watched a Pearl Harbor video. I remembered an *Adventures in Odyssey* episode about that called "East Winds, Raining." [46] My same-brothers were home from war and got married, but Stephen still fought to protect our country.

During the video, the new kid in class turned to me and hostilely said, "Why did you bomb us?" Then he smirked.

I screamed, "I did not!" Then I buried my head in folded arms and felt like crying.

That got the teacher's attention. "What's going on?"

I explained what the new kid said. The teacher questioned him, and he said he was joking. It wasn't funny to me. Just because the enemy was Asian didn't mean I had anything to do with it.

I told the new kid, "I wasn't even born then, and I'm not Japanese." I felt like he insulted people who cared for me and loved me—like Mrs. Choi, the mother of my heart.

There was another incident with the new kid. We were sitting on a gym bleacher. He was next to me and said, "You have n----r lips."

I reacted and pushed him. He got mad and told the staff person. I tried to explain, "But he said the N-word to me!" The staff person wouldn't listen. This wouldn't be the last time I would have encounters with him.

Another incident happened in the gym locker room where I did a stupid thing reacting to my classmates, and Mom got called in by the vice-principal. She was fed up with me. Dad was still in South America. School was going downhill. I got grounded for a week and missed Game Day.

That's one place I enjoyed to infinity—Game Day on some Saturdays at the library. I rode my bike there, played games, enjoyed snacks and soda, and rode home when it finished. Game Day with other kids made me feel welcomed and happy. I hated when I missed it.

I didn't think my parents believed me when I was blamed for stuff at school. Some things weren't my doing. Other times I did stupid things, but now my parents weren't listening to me. I was fed up.

I needed a breather and made a plan to leave. I had almost $20—enough to last a while. I grabbed my wallet and phone then thought I better leave a note.

Then I remembered my sister left our family. My parents were heartbroken and never got over it. If I went through with this, they lose another child. That would have a massive effect and bring more pain. I couldn't do that after what they went through, and I still loved my family.

Time passed, and I felt better because I loved my parents, my room, my bike, and freedom when I could go to Game Day and the store. And, even though he lived far away, Stephen returned from war, so that was over as far as our family's part.

I turned eighteen—adult age, but I had to go through a series of tests. The law said, if my I.Q. was too low, I must have a guardian and be confirmed "incapacitated."

One test was with a psychologist. I sat across the desk from him, and my parents were behind me, but they weren't allowed to help. The psychologist asked me as part of the test, "Is Superman real?"

I was dumbfounded by this question. I looked back at my parents with a puzzled look and shrugged. "He doesn't know?" *Should this guy be in the looney bin?*

When all the testing was done, I was relieved. I didn't understand why this was happening because my I.Q. wasn't a big deal to me. I was like Pooh Bear [47]—not given a bother. My results showed I needed a guardian.

The sheriff came to our door, asked for me, and served papers notifying me of a court date. Serious business! Now we weren't just me and parents. This was "Hampshire vs. Hampshire."

The next step? Court with a judge, and I needed my own lawyer and must pay for it. My parents also had to pay for a lawyer because they were willing to become my guardians. I was glad because, otherwise, the court could choose someone else. That would be strange.

We met with our lawyers, and in May the court day arrived. When it was my turn, the judge cleared the courtroom for privacy. Then the judge said he wanted a jury, so one had to be assembled from the people waiting. It took a long time.

During our wait, the judge asked if I wanted to sit at the bench. I was extremely excited! I walked up there and sat down, and the judge put his robe on my shoulders—like a superhero cape. He handed me the gavel.

I said, "I sentence my parents to get me Chinese food when this is over," and I banged the gavel and returned to my seat. We had a good laugh.

The rest went fast because no one disagreed that I needed a guardian. The judge pounded his gavel. Done. He congratulated us, the lawyers shook our hands, then my parents had to carry out their sentence.

So, we ate at the Chinese buffet, and it seemed we were the same because we were family; but now my parents must carry court papers, make decisions, and sign my documents because I was declared "incapacitated." This word was strange to me, so wires didn't connect what that meant.

I didn't know then, but I would need my parents' help big time in the future.

When final court papers came, I was irate and angst because the judge checked off boxes saying I couldn't vote or drive. Not driving didn't bother me much. But voting? I was beyond ticked! Why couldn't I vote? For the next nine years, I bellyached about it.

Dear Superman,   *March 2011-2012*

You should've seen Min's expression when a psychologist asked him if you're real. It took every ounce of self-control not to split a gut. Of course, you know this since you see through walls, unless you were out leaping tall buildings that day. If so, here's what happened:

Because of Min's developmental disability and age of eighteen, the law required he have a guardian if his I.Q. tested below 70. It did. We got "the job."

With the official business completed, we were what we'd always been, minus multiple hundreds of dollars. The difference? We must carry proof Min needs our help.

Supe', what happened to the good ol' days when folks cared for their disabled "child" because it was the right thing to do? Here we were, crippled by laws and systems. But it wasn't over. Not really.

We must report annually to the court, completing forms on every aspect of Min's life. At the one-year mark, we forgot this requirement and were served papers to appear on contempt charges. Who knew bringing Min halfway around the world fifteen years earlier came with such "perks!"

Don't take us wrong. Min's worth it. Yet this seems rather impersonal, but that's our life from "Happy birthday, eighteen-year-old!" until he dies or we do, raising another issue. What happens to Min if we go first? A stand-in guardian can be assigned. Back to court to add that.

Hey, Superman, you were adopted. Wait. You're not real. Or are you? We'll ask Min.

> *From citizens against kryptonite,*
> *Min's parent-guardians*

Then a sadness happened worse than my bellyaching. Dad's brother, my Uncle Rick, died. We were supposed to celebrate Grandma's ninety-fifth birthday. Instead, she buried her son. *This must be very hard to do.* I felt compassion for her, my Aunt Shannon, and cousin. I bought Grandma a little stuffed kitten to comfort her. And when I saw Dad cry, I tried to comfort him too.

It wasn't long until a new problem occurred. In school I hyperventilated. The nurse called my parents. "You'd better come for Min. His heart's racing and his blood pressure's way off."

Dad and Mom came right away, and we zoomed to the emergency room. The ER doctor didn't find anything wrong, but he said I should see a cardiologist—adding to my list of doctors.

The cardiologist did tests. By this time, it was summer break and I had to wear a 48-hour heart monitor. It didn't show anything. Next, I needed to wear one for a week. I also had to see our family doctor.

When I saw Dr. Mark, he said, "I'm concerned about this episode with heart racing and the continuing headaches. I'm scheduling an MRI of the brain because of that growth spotted in the midbrain three years ago."

The MRI happened June 28th, 2011. They used contrast dye, and I broke out with hives big time. I itched like crazy! Mom put cream on the hives but didn't think about my legs because I always wore jeans.

I didn't like shorts because I felt like my legs were cut off. Jeans helped me feel full legs. My parents didn't understand because it was summer, even though they knew more about Asperger's now.

I also had to be monitored because I couldn't tell if I was too hot or too cold, so I sat in my room and sizzled. I only had a fan in there. My parents gave me a thermometer and marked it. They said, "If the temperature reaches that mark, you must come downstairs."

But I neglected to look at it and baked. This worried my parents massively, so they set a timer every day and called, "What does the thermometer say?" I told them, and they said whether to come down or not.

Soon, I was going to another camp in Ohio because Camp KYSOC stayed closed. I went to Dr. Mark for a physical.

He checked me over, pushed my pant legs up, then shook his head. "What happened here?"

"I itched like crazy and didn't mean to do that." I lowered my head.

"I'm sorry. I can't sign this consent. Not with these open wounds."

I was disappointed. So were Mom and Dad, but I told them, "This will give you more time to enjoy me." The camp sent our deposit money back, and my parents bought a used PlayStation 2 to occupy me.

I liked "Metal of Honor" about war. My brothers were an inspiration because I learned we can't let the enemy conquer nations—like the game showed.

| 20 |

The Final Straw

"I'm sorry to say so, but sadly, it's true—That bang-ups and hang-ups can happen to you." —Dr. Seuss [48]

I started eleventh grade. The new kid was still in my class, but he wasn't new anymore.

During this year my teacher told my parents I smelled bad. They got after me about taking better care of myself. I never did this very well.

We also went to the dentist again. I always had many cavities. The dentist said so much was going on in there that she wanted to put me to sleep and fix all my teeth at the one-day surgery center. So that's what we did, like once before.

My teeth were fixed now, but I still smelled. Nothing seemed to help, even though my brushing improved and I had enough baths. This was bothersome. I couldn't tell that I smelled bad, so I didn't understand. I just smelled like me.

Our class was responsible for washing lunchroom tables, mopping the floor, and taking trash out after all the grades finished lunch. We took turns with jobs to teach us work skills. I didn't do very well. The aide and teacher made me repeat my jobs. I couldn't see any problem, just like I couldn't tell I smelled. *They're just harassing me.*

I complained to my parents, but they said, "You probably aren't doing a good job because you don't do well at home."

"But I do it, and you pay me," I argued.

"And we usually make you do things twice. We don't mind paying you if you do well," Mom said.

"Hmm. Maybe it's better if I don't work. It would save you and Dad money."

Mom rolled her eyes.

One day after we cleaned the lunchroom, it was my turn to take trash out with another kid. We threw the bags in the dumpster then got distracted and forgot to go inside. The other kid wrote in the dumpster dust with his finger. I enjoyed watching him. We both got in trouble, and my parents were called again.

A lunchroom poster showed how to do the Heimlich maneuver. The not-new-anymore-kid grabbed me by the throat and choked me. I wasn't sure if he meant to or if he was doing the Heimlich maneuver because one step showed a hand on someone's throat.

I had a hard time swallowing for a few days. It felt painful. My parents were angst and angry, and Dad called the school to complain about this and the kid.

I felt anxious in school until a meeting with the teacher, my parents, and me to figure out a regular class I could attend for the rest of the year. Someone mentioned landscaping, taught by the same teacher who did other jobs classes. I had him half of the year but wasn't allowed to take part—only watch.

Mom piped up, "Min might do well with landscaping." She looked at me. "You're really strong."

"Hmm, I might like that."

Actually, I loved it! We took care of the school landscape, but I wasn't allowed to use power tools—like the other kids. An aide took me, stayed, then walked me back to class. Except for the aide being there, it felt like freedom but not really.

But there was still Game Day for freedom when I wasn't in trouble. And no aide went with me, and I could ride my bike.

Back in the special ed room more trouble brewed. During free time, we could use school laptops to watch cartoons. The rules were strict.

One day I went on YouTube to watch a "SpongeBob SquarePants" video.[49] It said "edited." *Oh, it's shorter.* I clicked on it. I didn't wear headphones, but it was pretty quiet. I knew "SpongeBob" episodes, but this was different. All of a sudden, I heard super bad words. *Did they really say what I think they said?*

Another student overheard the video and snitched. The teacher had me bring the laptop to her desk. She watched a little then sent me to the office. The vice-principal looked too, and he was disappointed in me.

My parents got another call, saying I broke the rules watching something with curses. The laptop was taken away for a week.

My nineteenth birthday arrived. I already reached "age of majority," which means eighteen or over but still in school. I could read fourth-grade level, although formerly my reading level was higher.

Math was a different story. I only reached second-grade level, even though everybody thought I would be this math genius when I was a wee lad because I was a phenomenal counter and loved numbers to infinity and back—a never-ending straight path in space with no U-turn.

My birthday was good, but I still had school troubles. Other times I got kicked in the knee by a person wearing boots, hit in the head, and karate kicked in the kidney. I didn't get blamed for these, but they hurt like kingdom come!

My parents didn't tolerate this. Dad went into school and said, "If you don't stop this bullying, we're taking our son out!"

Lots of mornings I told Mom I didn't feel good and should abandon school. She said no. I kept asking because I really didn't feel good in the morning, but Mom kept it up too.

My parents thought my sick-feeling was caused by stress from bullying—especially the not-new-anymore-kid. I was also sick of my teacher complaining I smelled bad and my parents hassling me about brushing my teeth better.

There was a meeting that spring about my future, even though I had one more year of school. Another lady came and talked about vocational training when I graduated. I could take tests to see about attending the state disability training center. *This might be a good idea!*

My parents took me at the end of April to visit there. Seeing many different jobs interested me. *I can do this someday.*

The vocational lady scheduled me for tests to see what jobs I could do in the future even though that was a long time away.

May 2012. By now I stayed home alone up to three hours without difficulty. My parents worked on this goal for me.

The rules were, while I was alone, no answering the phone or the door. My cell phone must be on, and my parents put theirs on so I could call if there was an emergency. No cooking while they were gone because I ruined one microwave.

My parents needed to go to Lowe's across the river by the Dairy Queen where the dog ate the bottom of our ice cream cones.

Before this day, we had two tires slashed on different days. But today my parents were driving our car to Lowe's, so our carport was empty, and I was safe at home with the dog and cat. My phone was on. I went downstairs for a snack. I glanced out the kitchen window and saw the not-new-anymore-kid in our carport.

He had a bat—not like a bat in the sky—a metal baseball kind. He saw me and threatened, "If you tell anyone I was here, I'll come back for you and your family!"

Inside myself I was terrified. I unlocked the pantry door where the dog was and hugged her. She licked me. I didn't call my parents. *I better keep my mouth shut because this kid is capable of harm.*

When my parents got home, they sensed something was off. Mom asked, "What's bothering you?"

I started to cry. "The not-new-anymore-kid was here. He had a bat."

"A bat? What was he doing with it?" Mom asked.

"Tapping it on his shoulder and saying stuff."

Dad became agitated. "What kind of stuff?"

I thought I didn't handle my situation right, so I spilled almost everything. "He threatened to hurt us." But I kept some thoughts inside. *The kid will kill us if I say more.*

Mom looked worried. "Why didn't you call us?"

"I don't know." *If I let out my feelings, we'll be killed.* That's what I thought the not-new-anymore-kid meant. I knew I could trust the dog. She was an ear-witness to it all, but I knew she wouldn't talk.

Dad got the police involved. He had enough of the bully hurting me and thought that kid slashed our tires. I asked the not-new-anymore-kid later, and he said he did it.

My parents were scared for my safety. And worse? He ruined my freedom. Dad said, for a while, I should be driven places. The bully might retaliate if he saw me riding my bike. And I couldn't be home alone.

I felt disoriented and devastated. I was still free, but it didn't feel the same.

Eleventh grade would end soon. Dad went to the school superintendent to talk about homeschool for twelfth grade, but he learned more. Because I had enough credits and reached "age of majority," I could graduate a year early, which was now. *Great news! If only I can make it until graduation.*

The principal, my special ed teacher, and us three met about this plan. We sat around a big conference table like people use at important meetings.

Dad said, "We understand Min has the option to graduate at the close of this year."

"That's correct," the principal said. "We've reviewed his records, and he's met the state requirements needed to receive his Certificate of Completion (ee) and is also the age of majority."

"Then this is what we want to do," Dad said.

A dream come true even though I never dreamed it! I asked the principal, "Can I have a cap and gown?"

"We'll see. They've already been ordered, but there may be an extra."

Then I asked, "Can I be in the graduation photo of us all making the number twelve?"

"That can be arranged," he said.

I turned to my parents, "I'm going to be in the number twelve picture!" My face smiled.

Everyone signed the documents. Done.

May 27th, 2012 would be my graduation day! We quick planned a party and mailed invitations. I wanted to invite my landscape teacher —the only one from school I hoped would come.

Mom shopped for party supplies. We even got pencils with graduation cap erasers!

Then something really troublesome happened. We were in small groups in a random classroom, having a competition. Whatever group got the most points won. I worked on a puzzle for my group. We were timed. I was good at puzzles, but this one challenged me.

I very concentrated on it, but someone kept moving pieces. This changed my perspective. I couldn't handle it. I didn't ask the person to stop. Instead, I went into overload. I pounded my fist on my knee when time was almost up. Then, I didn't realize it, but I bent my arms up and shook my fists in the air near myself because time ran out.

The teacher saw and motioned for me to come to her. She said I threatened harm because I shook my fists. I tried to explain I was frustrated and didn't know I did it. But she wouldn't listen, put me between her and an aide, and marched me toward the office.

On the way, the teacher asked the aide, "Do you agree that Min shouldn't be in the graduation photo?"

"Yes."

When we got to the vice-principal's office, the teacher said I should be punished by not being allowed in the graduation number photo. He agreed.

I was broken. I reached my limit! *I'm leaving! What's the point of staying if I can't be in that photo!* I marched toward the office door that went outside.

Then I stopped. Would I get in trouble at home if I did this? I also needed to cross a very busy road. I didn't know if I could do it without help, so I stayed.

FYI:

(ee) For high school graduates who cannot earn traditional diplomas

| 21 |

Unforeseen Circumstances

"For I know the thoughts, that I have thought towards you,
saith the Lord ... thoughts of peace, and not of trouble,
to give you an end, and your hope." Jeremiah 29:11 [50]

When school let out that day, I went to the car but didn't get in front like usual. Instead, I opened the sliding door and dove into the middle seat, buried my head into the dog, and wrapped my arms around her.

Mom saw the vice-principal approaching the car and snapped—not like snapping her fingers! "Oh no! What's happened now?"

"I don't know." I stayed in the comfort of our dog.

When the vice-principal reached the car, Mom only put the passenger window down a little and listened to him blab about how I threatened harm with my fists.

Mom just said, "We'll deal with this at home," and pulled away. She didn't say another word.

I heard crying sounds, and that made me cry too.

At home Mom got out and slammed the door.

Me and the dog figured we were in big trouble because her tail was between her legs. She went to her bed like always when she was disobedient.

I put my backpack away and unpacked my lunch containers to be washed.

Mom distraughtly told Dad, "I can't face that man anymore! I couldn't even look at him."

"I'll pick up Min from now on." Then Dad called me.

I went into the living room and sat facing my parents. Mom told Dad what the vice-principal reported. Dad steamed like a tea kettle, but he listened as I explained my side of the story. Then he steamed more and told me to go upstairs. I did but listened through the vent because I knew this wasn't over.

I heard Dad say, "Are you kidding me? A special ed teacher who's supposed to understand Asperger's thought that was a threat? Even WE know kids with autism shake their fists when they're frustrated!"

I breathed a sigh of relief. Now I fully understood my parents were allies. I heard phone noise and Dad talking to someone. Then he called another person and let them have it.

The next day at school, the vice-principal met me in the hallway. I hesitated.

He apologized for misunderstanding the day before. I forgave him and went to class. The aide also said she was sorry. I forgave her too. The teacher didn't say anything.

I started my work as usual. Then someone knocked on the classroom door. In walked Dad. *Why is Dad here?*

He walked in toward the teacher's desk and stopped. "Have Min get all his belongings. I'm taking him home." Then he told me, "Get your stuff."

I did. I realized I wasn't coming back. I didn't care, but I hugged certain people goodbye.

I ate Doritos when I got home. Cool Ranch flavored. Sort of a sad celebration. When I was a fifth-grader in the mountains, Blake shared Doritos with me to help me cope and succeed.

At the age I am now, Blake wrote, "I love Min … I always tried to make sure he felt loved and included." That did help me.

I confessed to my parents I wanted to walk out of school that week.

They said they would've supported my decision—that they would feel like walking out too if they were me.

The next Monday I didn't need to go to school. I wouldn't anyway because I was having a belly ultrasound to check my kidneys because of my NF1 and blood pressure issues.

I had my ultrasound, but we didn't leave. I worked on the Scooby-Doo monster drawing I started in school. Nightmare Wrath had mixed-up body parts, goat mask, and tank hidden under his black robe with a tube down his sleeve. When he lifted his hand, hallucinogenic gas "thhht-ed" his victims.

While we waited, I told the technician about other Scooby monsters I invented and the infinity number of lists I had.

Then the radiologist came in and showed my images.

I focused on my drawing until Mom gasped and said, "Oh my word!" That got my attention.

I had a tumor under my left kidney—bigger than an orange but smaller than a regular-sized grapefruit. He said it needed to come out.

We ate on the way home. My parents asked if I understood the results, except they didn't talk with food in their mouths. They swallowed first.

Sounded like I needed an operation. *How did this tumor get there? Did the kick I got in the kidney at school cause this?*

Tuesday, we returned to the hospital for more tests. Afterward, we shopped at Best Buy. Dad got a laptop computer. I wondered why because he already had one.

When we were home again, the hospital called and said come for more tests on Wednesday and bring suitcases. *Oh no! We're staying?*

The next morning, I had a chest x-ray and another big test. They injected radioactive substance into me, and we waited for it to go through my whole body. Then they took me into the PET-scan room and put me on the table. The technician strapped me down.

"Help! I've been captured by enemy forces and injected with truth serum!" I told my parents. "I'm an alien lifeform, and they're holding me against my will!"

The technician laughed and finished getting me ready. "You're quite a joker."

"You can't make me talk. You won't get info out of me." I laughed to myself. *I'm nineteen human years but maybe 19,000 alien years. They're experimenting on me!*

But inside I emoted apprehension, fear, and nervousness. I had to lay still longer than I ever did in my whole life because they scanned me from head to toe. They gave me sedation medication.

While we waited for results, a clown came and spinned a plate on the end of a stick and balanced a peacock feather on her fingertip. She let me keep the feather. I loved this and tried to do the tricks too, but I couldn't. It gave us a good chuckle, though, on a hard day waiting.

The doctor finally came and talked with my parents, then I was assigned to a room. We got me settled in. A lady came and told me about the playroom. I could play there or bring toys to my room—like a toy library or being locked in Toys-R-Us! I wanted to check it out!

Along the way, I passed rooms with kids and their parents. Some kids had no hair. In one room a baby cried all the time. One rule in that ward: I couldn't visit in other rooms, but I could wave to kids from the hallway. So I did, and some waved back.

I could order my meal. I got a cheeseburger with fixin's, fries, and a Sprite. Then no more food because I was having surgery the next day.

That night Mom went to a cancer Lodge to sleep. Dad stayed, and we had our own little sleepover.

| 22 |

Complete Craziness

"Mine help cometh from the LORD ... He will not suffer
thy foot to slip: for He that keepeth thee, will not slumber."
Psalm 121:2-3 [51]

The next morning Mom showed up with a box and handed it to Dad.

Dad said, "Put your paper and pencils away for a while."

So I did.

He put the box on my bed table.

I remembered Monday we stopped at Best Buy and knew what this was. "Is that for me?"

Dad unpacked it while Mom explained, "This is an early graduation present from Jeff and Marion. It'll keep you busy."

Mom and Marion worked together in deaf ministry many years ago. Jeff and Marion cared about our family and sent me special things. It felt touching that they did this. It was the nicest thing anyone ever gave me.

Dad set it up, and my fingers flew in the air waiting to land on those keys. I was so excited—like Scooby-Doo craving Scooby Snacks! But I couldn't eat because I was waiting for surgery, so I looked up food on the Internet.

The playroom lady visited to see if I wanted some toys. I did. She brought them to me, which was easier because I had an IV now.

This day in the hospital I was preoccupied. Everything was good except the no-food business.

There wasn't an operating room available until supper. The nurse said we could choose surgery then or in the morning. We chose morning, so I ate. I was full and happy, and I wanted to use my new laptop all night.

It was Mom's turn to sleep over. She wouldn't let me stay up too late.

Early the next morning, I went for surgery. My parents stayed with me a while. I was terrified I would wake up during surgery with my belly cut open. I became frantic and panicked.

The anesthesiologist said, "I promise you won't wake up. I'll make sure."

Nervousness made me talk-talk-talk, like a madman, but the medical people were nice and talked-talked-talked back with me—like a bunch of mockingbirds—until they put the mask on me and asked me to count. That's the last thing I remember.

When I woke up, I was like a zombie, but I didn't want flesh. After the nurses knew I was okay, they moved me to the recovery room. I told jokes, but I winced in pain. My blood pressure rose higher and higher, and I couldn't leave until it dropped.

Dear Letter "O", Number 3, (ff) and All People Who Sing in German,

Our apologies for all the tissues recovery room nurses needed today. No, they weren't crying. Instead, they laughed themselves to tears.

We were shown to Min's bedside in a large room with multiple beds. We expected Min to be groggy and in pain—not loopy!

"Miss, Miss!" he called, holding a doughnut-shaped pillow on his belly."

"Yes?" the nurse replied.

"Knock, knock."

"Who's there?" asked the nurse.

"Who."

She smiled. "Who who?"

"What are you? Some kind of owl? That's funny, right?"

"Very." The nurse laughed.

"I got another one," Min said.

Brian placed his hand on our son's forehead. "Min, you've got to rest. We need your BP to drop."

"Okay." He became restless. "Miss, Miss."

"Yes?" She attended to him again.

"Sorry. I'll rest now."

"That's fine." The nurse checked his stats then updated those readings. Min's blood pressure rose more. "Miss, Miss. Just one more?"

"Sure." She stepped away from the computer and came to Min's side.

"Why didn't the puppet cross the road?"

"I don't know." She attempted to contain herself.

"Because he needed a hand. 'Get it?'"

"Yes. That's funny." She grabbed a tissue and blotted her cheeks.

Min lifted the pillow off his belly and handed it to Brian. "It's a doughnut!"

"Or an 'O,'" Brian added. "This program's brought to you by the letter 'O.'"

"And the number three!" Then Min announced with gusto, "Let's all sing!" He waved his finger as if directing. "In German!"

With that his nurse completely lost it! She grabbed more tissues. Other nurses attempted to compose themselves. The whole recovery room became comedy central.

Hopefully, the nurses regained control once Min left. By the way, they handled his care wonderfully. And what did they gain? A wider repertoire of jokes, which we can't imagine will come in handy.

So, letter "O"—Operation Over. Number 3—Three Times longer in recovery. And all people who sing in German—Das ist alles.

Attempting to compose ourselves,

the comedian's parents

Eventually, I was returned to my room. I had lots of tubes and wires. The thing down my throat hurt most. I wanted it out, but the nurse said, "Not yet." I kept my head turned right to cope. I tried to look down and touch my incision.

My parents said, "Leave it alone."

I put my head back and just laid there. This felt like the worst possible thing to happen, but my situation would turn more problematic.

A male nurse assigned to me introduced himself. "My name is C___."

My voice was raspy and deep, and my mouth was dry. "That's the same name as this bully from school." It hurt something fierce to talk, but I had to get this out. "He came to our house and threatened my family." *This C___ is a nice, innocent one. He isn't like the not-new-anymore-kid.*

Mom and Dad took turns eating at the special parents' room because no outside food was allowed into this ward. Dad got supper and ate because he was spending the night. When he got back, Mom left to eat and sleep at the Lodge.

Dear Barnes & Noble Bookseller,   *May 25th, 2012*

You looked rattled when I answered your "may I help you" with sobbing.

"I need the best kids' joke book you've got!"

You took me to a lovely all-things-children section, not knowing this was for someone graduating high school in "four sleeps." But things weren't what they were "supposed to be."

Wednesday, when we met with a surgeon after Min's tests, we learned his tumor was suspicious. We asked if that meant malignant.

He answered, "We won't know for sure until it is biopsied."

Min was assigned a room in the cancer wing. When a social worker said we parents were eligible to stay at the American Cancer Society Lodge nearby, another piece of this nightmare rattled us.

Brian and I decided we'd take turns with Min. Wednesday night—Brian, Thursday—me, tonight—Brian.

Just this morning, the chief neurosurgeon performed Min's surgery. Now our son lay post-op in horrible pain. NF1—you cruel disease!

My night "off." I'd make the hour trip home to care for pets and bring in mail. I started driving home when events of the whole week caught up with me and my tears flowed.

I decided to stop at your bookstore and knew exactly what I'd buy.

It was then, Mr. Bookseller, I charged in toward you, and you asked "May I help you?" And you did.

Jokes were Min's trademark. He'd tell one, then ask, "Was that funny?" And if someone told him one, he'd also ask, "Was that funny?"

I picked a huge book with 5000 jokes. [52] "This will do." I wiped away tears. "Thank you so much."

When I arrived home, I asked a neighbor to care for pets and collect mail until Min's release Wednesday. Then I returned to the Lodge, hoping for a good night's rest. I looked forward to giving Min the joke book when I'd relieve Brian.

And that's the story, Bookseller. Thank you for your help. Our son's gonna LOVE this book, but I'll likely regret buying it.

Sincerely,

a satisfied customer

P.S.—Saturday, 5:30 a.m. Awoke early and couldn't fall back asleep. Sunrise. Might as well head to the hospital and put the joke book on Min's bed table for when he wakes up!

I wasn't eating. I laid there in and out of sleep and didn't give a care in the world.

That evening I became a troubled soul. In the wee night hours, I completely lost it. "He's here. He's going to attack me!" I cried.

Dad stayed nearby all this time. "Who's here?"

"C___'s here! He's coming at me! He's got the bat, and he's going to kill us!" I tried to stop him by pulling my tubes and wires and clawing my incision.

Dad hit the call-nurse button.

"Yes?"

"I need help! Min's going to hurt himself!"

A nurse zoomed in and called for backup. More help arrived, and the next few hours it took several people to hold me down. The nurses who helped started crying.

Then a nurse put a drug into my IV, and I began to calm and fall in and out of sleep. But every time I woke up, I told Dad the bully was still there. Dad kept his hand on my forehead. It usually comforted me, but now it only slowed my anxiety because the bully wouldn't leave.

People surrounded my bed. I didn't know who they were or if they were real, but they must have come to remove the bully.

It was still night, and I dosed off.

When I opened my eyes again, some light shined in the window, and Mom was standing next to Dad by my bedside.

My head was still turned right, but I could see her in my peripheral vision. Turning my head left was too painful, but I had to tell Mom! "The bully was here! He tried to kill us!"

"Don't worry. He can't come back. Security officers downstairs won't let him in the elevator, and we won't leave you alone."

"But he was here," I said with distress. Mom tried to convince me I was safe, but I knew it wasn't so because I saw him.

FYI:

(ff) Referencing "Sesame Street"—PBS children's program

| 23 |

"Rappy Raduation!"

"... God has shown me that my experience is to be used
to help others ... one heart knows when
another heart is aching." —Doris Van Stone (foster child)[53]

The bully left, and I breathed relief. Dad got ready to leave. He told Mom he was going to the police about the bully, so Dad was my hero.

Now I was safe.

Mom's turn to stay.

The rest of Saturday I slept on and off. I tried to do computer, but I felt miserable. Watching cartoons on TV distracted me, but all I really wanted was the tube out of my throat.

To the evil one sending the nightmare from the abyss,   *May 26th, 2012*

I just spent the night with our son writhing in terror. How dare you perpetrate such a reprehensible act on our vulnerable boy!

Min's assigned nurse had the same name as the school bully. Did you design that into your evil plan?

During Min's inconsolable, drug-induced state of mind, a doctor, nurse, psychologist, social worker, clergywoman, and distraught father seemed powerless to help.

I'd known Min was upset about the bully, but I hadn't fathomed the depth of his silent suffering until drugs released all restraint and he vocalized his terror.

Sarah arrived at sunrise. Her expression fell at the sight of people surrounding Min's bed. She tossed a book onto the bed table by the wall and came quickly to my side.

I shook as I told her what happened. Then we exchanged places.

I was totally spent but drove the hour home and went directly to the Chief of Police. I told him about last night—also that I'd previously filed complaints with his department and court social worker and confronted the school superintendent—to no avail.

The Chief apologized and said his hands were tied because of the school's pending action and social-worker involvement. I reminded him of our slashed car tires and the bully's threat with the bat. He assured me he'd send a patrol car frequently down our street.

Meanwhile, Min's suffering continued. Some staff eyed us as terrible parents, allowing our son to be traumatized. We were both questioned by the psychologist. And you, evil one, smiled.

Our son's physical recovery needs time. His mental and emotional recovery? Undoubtedly longer. But knowing and trusting God, your Adversary, assures us you won't win. Ultimately good will defeat evil.

Covered in God's armor,

warrior father

Sunday—May 27th, 2012. The sun shined in my hospital window. Mom woke up and got ready for the day. Dad would come from the Lodge soon.

I was stuck in bed with the tube still down my throat and a long fresh incision down my belly. During surgery, my intestines were moved to get to that small-grapefruit fibroma that grew because of NF1.

Through the whole nightmare, I was on overdrive. Now my body was a physical mess, and my mind was troubled. "Can you sit on the other side so I can see you better?" I asked in a whisper Mom heard.

"Sorry. With your monitor constantly beeping, the nurses need that clear." She stood up and leaned over the bed a little. It helped.

"What's today?"

"Sunday."

"Oh." I was quiet for some minutes. "My graduation day?"

Mom hesitated. "Yes."

Then my mouth went agape, and I wanted to cry, but no tears came.

This day was supposed to be way more different. I looked forward to participating in my graduation. My teacher already took away me being in the '12 graduation photo. I wanted that restored, but now it wouldn't happen.

The principal came through with a cap and gown before I went to the hospital. I put them on, and Dad took my picture and made special graduation announcements with me on front. Now the cap and gown hung at home, and I was in hospital garb instead.

We planned to have a party in our carport. I helped Mom hang long curtains on a rope to make it fancy and string Asian lanterns across the beams. It was going to be very special.

My parents also bought a graduation autograph book. Now? No signatures.

Just then Dad walked in and came to my bed. He saw my downcast face and looked at Mom with concern.

"We've been talking about graduation. I'll make another trip home and get some of the party stuff for a mini-ceremony." Mom looked at me. "How 'bout that idea?"

"I don't know."

"Sounds good," said Dad, "and, Min, I think you're getting company this afternoon." He rolled the bed table over, fired up my laptop, and put it slightly crooked so I didn't need to turn my head much. "There must be something on here you'll enjoy."

My attention went digital as Mom waved 'bye. I watched the video about Moses from *The Greatest Adventure—Stories of the Bible* [54] on YouTube for my church lesson. Me and Moses had stuff in common—we were both adopted and going through difficult times.

That afternoon Mom returned as my same-brothers arrived with their wives and two little nephews in a stroller.

On the wall under the TV was a whiteboard and marker. Michael drew a cartoon monkey and wrote "Min-key" by it.

I started to laugh, but it hurt so badly. "Stop. Don't make me laugh."

Then Nathan drew a cap and gown on the monkey. It was hard to smile and laugh but hard not to also.

Mom took my nephews to the gift shop. I just laid there while my same-brothers and Dad talked to cheer me up.

A while later Mom came back with the tots and balloons, and it was time for my graduation ceremony. "You'll have to wait for your cake. We couldn't bring it in, but it'll keep till you come home."

Dad cleared my bed table, and Mom set a little Scooby-Doo holding a rolled-up diploma at one end. She rubber-banded a plastic mini-graduation cap (from my cake) to the back of my left hand so two fingers could walk across the table. I couldn't do it, so Mom helped me.

My family members sang—"dum-dahdahdah-dum-dum, dum-dahdahdah-dum," a famous graduation song, *(gg)* while my fingers marched toward Principal Scooby-Doo. He handed my fingers the diploma and said, "Rappy Raduation!" *(hh)*

Dad moved the tiny tassel from one side to the other. I was now officially graduated. He unrolled the little diploma. It said "YOU DID IT!" And I did! Everyone got pencils with graduation cap erasers—family, nurses, doctors. Me too!

Even though I couldn't enjoy it all, I had support. My same-brothers cared a lot to come all that way for me. Only Stephen couldn't because he was in Colorado, but I had good news in my mind. I would see him in the summer.

After my siblings, their wives, and tots left, two friends Dad met at Raceway Ministries [55] visited. Dad called many people before my surgery asking for prayer. These guys prayed and came to encourage us. My parents needed some happiness, and this boosted their emotions.

For days after my surgery, I didn't improve. I was sent for x-rays to see if the tube down my nose and throat shifted, but it didn't. My blood pressure skyrocketed, even with proper medication.

On June 2nd the nurses slid me onto a gurney and wheeled me to put in a PICC line. [ii] Dad and Mom dressed in full hospital garb and waited outside while nurses took me in and moved me onto the table.

I told jokes because of my anxiety. The nurses joked back, and this helped me relax a little. They called in my parents. Ready to go!

I freaked! I was getting something else inserted in me—not just into my arm but up my arm across my chest to near my heart. I wanted out of that place! I was sedated but not put to sleep. I had to lay perfectly still or be put under.

Dad asked, "Could I talk to Min a minute?"

The nurse said, "Yes."

Dad focused on my eyes. "Listen, buddy. You need to be like a robot so you can get better. We don't want them to put you out. That would be too hard on you right now."

I listened, then my arm was numbed. But I freaked again, so my parents helped the nurses. Dad held down my top half with another nurse, and Mom laid across my legs to keep me from kicking. They said calming things to me.

It wasn't long until it was done.

After this I started improving, but my blood pressure stayed high. My nephrologist ordered a medicine patch to stick on the middle of my back below my neck. I needed this for months. It worked when it stayed put, but I was annoyed by it—like a scratchy shirt label.

When my surgeon visited, he explained my tumor had some active cells. They were removed. I wouldn't need chemotherapy. My tumor grew around things inside me, but he freed it. He said it wasn't jagged like hundreds of NF1 fibromas he removed—that my tumor came out like a ball.

My current self wanted to understand this better. I looked at my rock collection and picked two specific ones. One was rough and jagged with bumps. *That's what my tumor looked like before my surgery.* Then I looked at a smooth ball-shaped one and compared them. They weren't the same at all.

From Monday to Wednesday the week of surgery, tests showed my tumor looking like the rough, jagged, bumpy rock. My surgery was supposed to be Thursday, but it was postponed. Friday my fibroma looked like the smoother, ball-shaped rock and was easier for the surgeon to remove.

God changed it! I wonder now if the delaytion of my surgery was because God was at work, changing that nasty tumor.

It's similar to Lazarus' story.[56] Lazarus died. I didn't die. That's different. His sisters wanted Jesus to heal him when he was sick. They sent a message, but Jesus waited two days. Lazarus' sisters didn't understand that, but God knew what would transpire. When Jesus came, He cried. I don't know why. Maybe He felt sympathy for the on-lookers.

Then Jesus told dead Lazarus to come out, and he did. He was alive and didn't stink from death. This showed God's power. Jesus waited until Lazarus smelled bad so people wouldn't make false accusations saying Lazarus wasn't actually dead.

My surgery was delayed, and God changed my tumor. I didn't question why He didn't remove it fully because the surgeon cut it out, so it was gone anyway. And a good thing happened! The bad stink I had that school year was gone!

God knew what was good for me. There was a reason I went through this. I didn't know why then, but it doesn't matter. He knew I needed to be here. Maybe in Heaven, I can ask Him why He chose this method.

Beloved Son,   *May 31ˢᵗ, 2012*

Six sleeps ago you had surgery. You've suffered so much. Watching you go through this breaks our hearts.

A thought occurred as we stayed by your side: This is why we adopted you—so you wouldn't go through this alone. There were other reasons, but perhaps none more important as this (except for teaching you about the Savior).

Did we adopt you because we needed you? Not in one sense. Did we want you? Yes. We thought about what it might've been like if you faced this without family.

We've also reflected how our relationship with God, Who adopted us, is similar. Did He need us? Not really. Did He want us? Yes. And He's with us through joys and trials. We needn't go through anything alone.

During this struggle and horrible post-op, you cried, "I'm so glad you're here to help me."

Min, we are too, and we're grateful God is with us so we go through nothing alone.

With all our love,
Dad and Mom

I started getting better. On June 3ʳᵈ the nurse took the tube out of my throat, even though it felt like she was pulling a string of spaghetti out because I tried that when I was younger and did stupid things. Now I could waltz around with my IV pole, which kept beeping and driving everyone crazy. And I ordered food!

Mom and me went out in the hallway and walked a short way. I was weak and wobbly. When I got stronger, we walked around the ward because I wanted to see other patients.

As we walked down the hallway, I said, "I wonder why all these kids are here."

"They have cancer," Mom said.

"What! All of them?"

"Yes."

"Then why am I here?" I asked.

"Because they thought your tumor was cancerous, but the biopsy showed it hadn't turned what's called full-blown yet."

I looked in all the rooms as we passed. There were babies, toddlers, little kids—like my niece and nephews—and a teenage boy who I got to talk to from the doorway.

We stopped to rest, and I said, "I need to pray for these kids."

Looking back from my grown-up self, I wonder if that was my purpose for being there. Maybe I needed to know other kids suffered—I wasn't the only one. Like when the baby cried all the time. I was annoyed. "Can't that baby stop this business?" I didn't understand the baby had cancer and wasn't just having a fit. Possibly I wasn't there for me but for somebody else. The kids needed prayer. I could do that.

The rest of my wires and tubes became history. I was free! No IV pole! As we went down the hallway, I saw Dad coming. He smiled, seeing me up and walking free. I couldn't run to him but, when we reached each other, we hugged in open arms.

And that Monday afternoon, June 4th, I went home!

FYI:

(gg) "Pomp and Circumstance, March No. 1 in D" by Sir Edward Elgar

(hh) Scooby-Doo's pronunciation of "happy graduation"

(ii) "Peripherally inserted central catheter"

| 24 |

Signs and Symptoms

"God will help you through this ... It may be the darkness,
but ... if God has led you there, then that's where
He wants you to be ... Keep going!" —R.V. Fieker [jj]

At home, I opened my graduation presents from my parents—a small refrigerator and microwave. Mom planned to teach me to cook since I was done with school. This goal interested me.

Lots of people sent mail, and Mom made a large graduation cap box for cards. It was an exciting time!

I still had the blood pressure patch and needed to see the nephrologist.

Later I got my belly stitches out. That wasn't fun. The neurosurgeon said the small-grapefruit tumor could grow back, and he also saw a bunch of small fibromas on my aorta. I didn't know what that meant.

I liked learning to cook. Mom helped me make things in a small frying pan like grilled cheese or hot dogs, but the stove scared me. I could boil water in the microwave for ramen noodle soup though. Friends gave me a small George Forman grill. I could make cheeseburgers like real chefs.

I still wasn't back to my regular self. Two weeks later, I was in very bad shape. That scared my parents massively. In another two weeks, I bottomed out again. And when I sweated, the stupid patch fell off and my blood pressure spiked.

I wasn't out riding my bike because I needed to heal more and school was out. That meant the bully was too. So, me and Mom walked the dog around our little block, which was a square or rectangle.

On one of our walks, I asked Mom, "Did you ever have an invisible friend?"

"Nope. Do you?"

"I'm not sure. He doesn't talk to me."

"Maybe he's shy." She smiled.

"Oh," I said. "I wish he did talk because I want a friend."

"Well, you'll see Stephen soon. He's your friend. After all, he wouldn't give such an important job to just anyone!"

I smiled so big. We finished our walk right where we started.

Stephen asked me to be his best man. I wrote a speech to read at the party after the wedding. I was nervous about this assignment, but I wanted to do it wonderful for Stephen and his wife.

Before Stephen got engaged, he asked his future wife if she was willing for me to live with them if something happened to my parents. She said yes soul-heartedly. This showed extreme love that she cared so specially because I was a hard person to be dealt with.

The wedding was coming soon. I still wasn't my good old self, but my doctor okayed this best man to go. Imagine how awful it would be if I missed the wedding and the food!

Then a police officer came to our house and gave Dad papers to appear in court about the bully—the same date we were leaving for the wedding, and Dad was the wedding preacher. The court said show up or get charged with contempt. Dad had no choice. The bully messed things up and only got a "hand slap."

But the car was packed, so we vamoosed!

We stayed with Glenn and Karen, and I could go upstairs because I proved myself last time, but the grandpa was gone. He died.

We had a superb time in Colorado with family and friends.

I loved being able to ride my bike again. I could do that now because the bully was in school. And I rode to Game Day and didn't have the privilege taken away because school trouble was history!

In October I traveled with other teens to the vocational training center. We stayed over and took tests for different jobs. I wanted chef or childcare, but I didn't pass. I did okay with some others, but—when testing results came, it was not-so-good news.

Now what? We filled out papers with the vocational counselor. I needed to be approved to work at a place in town. I got accepted!

We visited that workshop. I was amazed! They had a soda machine and lots of paper! The boss and employees were nice and wanted me to join them.

I was responsible for packing my lunch every day. I liked that.

The weather was nicer now, so I rode my bike more, but I kept wrecking.

Both parents wanted to know about my bike-riding troubles. They said things like, "Why do you keep crashing?" and "You're not being careful!"

I told my parents I was blacking out and didn't mean to crash. For a while, they thought I was making excuses, but then we drove a long way to an eye specialist. The doctor said my eyes were fine. We got to eat on the way home.

I worked when there were things to do at the workplace. We did jobs for other businesses. When I got my first paycheck, I felt proud. We went shopping and on field trips too. My favorite was seeing a pro baseball game.

I wanted to ride my bike to work. I knew proper directions, like I learned my way to the library five years before. My parents thought this was a mixed-iffy situation because I was wrecking. I promised I would be more careful.

They said, "We'll see." But we didn't see because over the months I wrecked so much that my bike was ruined. I was now a twenty-year-old with my freedom gone.

My parents said, "You can do jobs, save your money, and buy another bike."

That's a good plan.

My parents showed me how to keep a paybook, and they would be like employers paying me once a week for jobs at home and for neighbors.

I liked earning money both places, but I wasn't a good saver.

Dad made a system for me with three different size cans screwed onto a board. Mom labeled them "tithe, savings," and "spending." They tried to help me figure ten percent for the tithe can, but I never understood. So they explained, when I earned $10.00, the tithe can got at least $1.00. They said, if I put $2.00 or more in the savings can, I would save enough for a nice bike in one year.

I can do that.

My parents told me we might move again. I hadn't been happy when I was in high school, but now I worked and had friends. I didn't want to go. But they said we'll move closer to my same-brothers because big news! Grandma was coming to live with us!

Dad fixed the house in case we didn't move before Grandma arrived. It took him more time to fix things now because he still had strokes every once in a while, and his hands didn't cooperate.

Mom took me on trips to the city an hour away to explore house ideas and some disability workplaces. Some were nice, so the idea started to sound good, and they had more Chinese restaurants and Asian markets!

We did this for a while, and we found a good place for me to work. By then we had our house all ready to sell or for Grandma— whichever happened first.

I still liked working in town, but I started getting dizzy and sick. Sometimes I fell. The staff called my parents to pick me up because they didn't want me injured on the job.

When we went to my next DDD appointment in August 2013, I was really out of it. The therapist said I needed to see my doctor, called him, and wheelchaired me to the parking lot. Mom took me.

I met this doctor the year before when Dr. Mark moved on. Dr. Tee knew all the Scooby-Doo episodes. My parents said that was nice, but it mostly mattered he was a good doctor; but he was a superb doctor and Scooby expert too! A magical combination!

"There's this episode where a ghost doctor smuggles gold in bread bags and scares everyone away from his operations," I told Dr. Tee.

"Right! So he isn't found out." He laughed and slapped his knee.

I gave a devious look. "Does that doctor work in this hospital?"

"No way! We're good guys here."

This was helpful history because now Dr. Tee wanted me to have a brain MRI in his hospital.

We changed rooms at home because Grandma was coming soon. She had to be downstairs. My parents moved upstairs into my room because that's where their bed would fit. I moved into our little extra room next door.

Mom said, "I'm sorry you're smooshed in there."

"I don't mind. It's cozy, like sleeping in a tent." But it was impossible to fit all my stuff, so Dad made me a media area downstairs. Mom cleared her upstairs work area into a place I could cook and eat. It was like a mini-apartment.

My books fit on shelves above my new dining counter, but my favorite book of people's last names (that I read a lot) stayed by my bed with *The Action Bible* [57] which I loved because I could read it with very good understanding.

My toys fit under my bed. I shoved my stuffed animals underneath when they were in time-out! Sometimes I separated the dogs and cats because they fought.

September 2013. Time for my MRI.

Done.

Then Dad flew to New York to get Grandma's stuff and bring it by U-Haul. Grandma would arrive by plane with my cousin helping her in a few days. I could hardly wait!

Dad returned, and my same-brothers and a wife unloaded the truck and got Grandma's room arranged like a studio apartment. I would like visiting Grandma in this redone space.

We opened the box with the little kitty I gave her when Uncle Rick died. It was sitting well-behaved. Cats like boxes. I welcomed kitty and put it on Grandma's bed.

Grandma and my cousin arrived!

This was close to when Dr. Tee called about my MRI. He saw something. I had another MRI with contrast, and for sure something was growing deep in my brain.

My random children's hospital set up doctors' appointments. One with a neurosurgeon. One of those fixed my belly, but now I needed a head one. The other was with an oncologist. I didn't know what that was.

Dear Min's Bike,   *Autumn 2013*

You've had it rough since Min adopted you. He loved you, but now you're headed to the place where bikes go to die.

Min enjoyed the freedom you provided, riding you farther than he'd ever ridden.

Then he began crashing. He said he couldn't help it. His eyes were fine, so we assumed Min wasn't paying attention to where he was going.

I fixed you repeatedly. But too many hard hits brought us to the day I told Min, "I can't fix this bike anymore."

Min was "wheel-less." He could walk places but wasn't highly motivated. And after his abdominal surgery, he wasn't the same.

At his fall 2012 DDD appointment the therapist said, "This isn't at all like Min."

After filling her in on tests and appointments Min had, Sarah mentioned we needed another family physician because Dr. Mark moved on.

The therapist recommended another physician.

Soon after, Sarah and I took Min to Dr. Tee, located in another hospital. He and Min clicked right away. Dr. Tee listened to our concerns, jotted notes, then reviewed those with us. We mutually agreed we'd see how Min did the next few months and return in early 2013.

Min's Bike, encouraging news! Dr. Tee adjusted your owner's medications, and Min seemed more his former self.

Late spring, we started preparing for my ninety-seven-year-old mother to come live with us. Sadly, though, we observed Min digressing.

While I readied for Mom, Sarah took Min to his end-of-summer DDD appointment. She called and relayed Min bottomed out, vomited repeatedly, and could barely walk. Sarah took him immediately to Dr. Tee.

He was shocked to see Min listless, treated him, and scheduled an MRI of the brain.

Min had that scan, then Mom arrived.

Several days later, Dr. Tee called. Results showed a suspicious area deep in the brain as well as the other tumor discovered in 2008. He ordered another MRI with contrast for a clearer look.

During the interim, Dr. Tee requested we gather previous MRI imaging, including the one Dr. Mark ordered at our local hospital in 2011.

These weeks of waiting seemed too great to bear. We hid our anxiety— Mom being unaware of Min's dire situation. But nights? Tears soaked our pillows.

Min's second MRI took place mid-October with results coming days later.

Dr. Tee confirmed the mass—strongly suspected of being a late-stage tumor. His colleagues agreed. He sent findings to Min's hospital.

Our hearts were in our throats. We couldn't breathe. We weren't over the shock when the children's hospital scheduled neurosurgery and oncology appointments for the following week.

Min's bike, in hindsight we realize your dings and damage weren't intentional. They were signs we failed to recognize. We're sorry. You deserved a nicer funeral, but right now we just can't bring ourselves to say goodbye.

Still in shock,

Min's Dad

FYI:

[jj] Pastor—Aurora Fundamental Methodist Church, Missouri—January 30th, 2022 a.m. sermon

| 25 |

Facing Death Head-On

*"Surely goodness and mercy shall follow me
all the days of my life ..." Psalm 23:6a* [58]

The appointments day arrived. Dad stayed with Grandma because she couldn't be alone. Me and Mom traveled to my random hospital.

At the first appointment, the nurse did all the nurse stuff. Then she let me watch a movie while Mom went across the hall.

I picked a random movie, and I took out my paper and pencil to make lists. They left the door open.

I hadn't watched even half the movie when Mom came back.

She said shaky-like, "Get ready to go."

I pounded my fist. "But the movie isn't over yet. Can I please watch to the end?"

"No, we've gotta boogie to the next appointment!"

I put my belongings in my backpack, and we vamoosed!

We walked far and fast. Then Mom said we needed a quick rest.

I went over and looked through a book cart and picked some books. They were free for patients. Sometimes I donated some.

Then Mom called me over to explain what just happened and what's in my head.

I had a new tumor, and it was big. *Why do I have this, and where did it come from?*

Mom said we needed to see a cancer doctor next.

I was shocked and confused, but I had to stay that way because we must hurry.

When we arrived at the appointment, a nurse called my name. She led us to a room, and I climbed onto the exam table.

This random doctor came in and introduced himself as Dr. Choo because that's who he was.

I opened my clipboard case and took out paper and a pencil to continue my list. A nurse stood by me. I overheard Dr. Choo tell Mom about brain tumors, cancer, and chemotherapy. I understood a little, but I didn't want it to go on, so I asked the nurse, "Do you like disco?"

"Hmm, I guess I do." She grooved a disco move.

"Do you own a disco ball?"

"No, but that'd be cool!"

"Spinning disco balls can cause people with epilepsy to have seizures. I don't have seizures."

Mom heard this crazy conversation. I gave her a little wave. I didn't know how sad she was, but disco-talk made her smile and shake her head.

We stayed a gracious amount of time.

Then Dr. Choo asked if I had questions.

"Can we leave now?" I looked what time it was. "It's way past lunchtime."

He smiled. "Certainly."

We went to Rally's and got cheeseburgers, curly fries, and soda. I liked going there because the drive-thru window was on the passenger side, and I could help pay.

Mom's voice had shakiness, and once in a while she sniffled; but she asked if I wanted to do anything else on the way home.

I picked Toys-R-Us because I had a deep interest—My Little Pony. Due to my trauma in high school, I looked for ways to cope back then. I wasn't still having nightmares, but I felt scarred inside.

There was something called Bronies—dudes who liked the Ponies. I liked that the Ponies taught friendship, kindness, loyalty, laughter— and I wanted a friend. I ended up making friends later, but at that moment in my life I felt alone and hurt.

Now I got bad news at the hospital, and I searched the Toys-R-Us My Little Pony display.

Mom placed her hand on my back. "How 'bout we buy one?"

"No thank you." I stared at all those Ponies. *If only I could buy you all to help me calm and cope!*

But I couldn't. I went home empty-handed.

Dear Goodness and Mercy,   *October 21ˢᵗ, 2013*

Help! A storm's hit, and we're already trudging a tear-soaked path!

You were there that dreaded day, but we couldn't see through the fog when I took Min to his neurosurgery and oncology appointments.

I hesitated when the neurosurgeon's nurse had Min choose a movie and send me across the hall, but I left him with his prerecorded babysitter.

There I sat, facing a large screen. Apparently, I'd see a "movie" too.

The nurse stood by a computer.

Then the neurosurgeon came in, introduced himself, and sat near me. After some brief niceties, the doctor asked the nurse to bring up MRI images onto the screen. Storm clouds billowed in wait.

As the nurse clicked, the doctor explained then requested she zoom in. The storm did also. "Two tumors—probable astrocytomas—"inoperable."

I stared at this "horror film."

He explained the mass deep in the brain crossed midline, which made it inoperable. "One option is partial resection, which is removing a small portion of the mass. The other is to biopsy. Either choice helps the oncologist determine the best chemotherapy regimen."

I couldn't speak. All I knew was the storm hit because my cheeks were wet.

"Mrs. Hampshire, you and your husband will need to decide what you want to do."

"You can't take the mass out?" The thunder apparently deafened.

"No. It has crossed midline."

This made no sense to me. Here I was—staring at images that changed everything. Our choices? There wasn't a good one. Either way, our son would eventually die.

I thanked him somehow and picked up Min from his medical cinema.

We started the long walk to our next appointment, which was in twenty minutes. I spotted a bench, told Min I needed to stop, and encouraged him to pick some books from a book cart. I usually suggested he take one or two. Today? I would've given him the world.

I called Brian and told him the news.

He groaned.

I asked him what I should tell Min in the next few minutes. For cryin' out loud, we were heading to oncology!

Brian suggested keeping it minimal.

I clung to that phone, not wanting to hang up, but I had to let my husband go.

I called Min over.

He sat on the bench and opened a book.

"Listen carefully. You can look at that later."

Min closed the book. His eyes wandered to passersby.

I gave him our routine "pay attention" indicator. "The doctor we just saw operates on heads."

"Am I going to have another operation? Can I order cheeseburgers and fries again?"

"We can't talk food now, but it looks like you will. We'll discuss all this later with Dad. Okay?"

"Yeah." He fidgeted with the books.

"Min, listen. The next appointment is with a cancer doctor."

"Do I have cancer?" He flicked the book edges.

I put my hand atop his, and he stopped. "I don't know. I just know that's what kind of doctor he is, and he wants to meet with us. Remember when we went over the MRI results at home?"

He nodded and clutched the book to himself. "Will I have that tube down my throat? Will the clown visit and do magic tricks? Remember when she was spinning the plate and ..."

"I can't answer all that now. We've gotta boogie to oncology, and it's pretty far." I stood up and grabbed the neurosurgery papers.

Min picked up his other books, and we continued our trek. If only we could reach the eye of the storm. Momentary peace, but no calm for now.

At oncology, a nurse led us to a room with an exam table on the right and a child-height table and chairs on the left. Cheery characters decorated the walls.

Dr. Choo came in and greeted us. He spoke gently.

Min's eyes darted about.

One nurse stood near Min, and another near me. Would I need a nurse?

The doctor joined me at the kiddie table and opened a folder of papers. He explained treatment possibilities, depending what type tumors Min had—also that all brain tumors were considered cancer of the brain and didn't spread to other parts of the body—differing from other cancers.

We'd return to talk about chemotherapy and learn when Min's medical port would be implanted after Min's brain surgery incision healed. He asked if I had questions and said we could call if any entered our minds.

He then addressed our son who mainly wanted out of there.

I wanted to flee home, but Min needed something positive. He chose our late lunch spot and a toy store visit. Releasing my tears must wait ...

... and wait longer once home. There was supper to prepare, eat, and clean up. Then Min went upstairs, and my mother-in-law watched her evening shows.

My mind, however, was fixed on the "horror movie" I'd seen earlier.

Once Mom headed to her room for the night, I collapsed with Brian and dumped everything.

He wailed.

I'd never seen him like this. Then I sobbed.

I don't know how long we wept, but we finally pulled ourselves together enough to call the boys. Nathan, then Michael—the eve of their shared birthday. Dump on them tonight? Yet they'd want to know. Then Stephen. All three wept.

Before we turned in, we both recognized something at the same time. Min needed us to walk him Home.

We faced this eighteen years ago when we "invited Min Soo to sit at our table," learned the possibility he had a fatal genetic disease, and planned to adopt him "even if he is going to die." Had that been a foreshadowing?

Goodness and Mercy, we're just sheep and don't know how to do this. Thankfully, your Shepherd guides us as we must now walk with our lamb who's been invited "to sit at God's table." (kk)

But our son doesn't understand. He's just a lamb and afraid of storms. "Why does everything happen to me? I want to hit something!"

"You can talk about it with us and God too," Brian said.

"But I really want to hit something!"

"We'll find a way to work through this, buddy." He held Min a while.

The next day, Brian planned to fill in his mom while Min and I ran errands.

Min requested we stop at our local thrift store.

I spotted throw pillows and recalled a pastor's wife years before telling me they had an adopted angry son, drew a face on a pillow, and let the boy punch it.

"Hey, Min!"

"Huh?" He glanced up from digging through a pile of stuffed animals.

I picked up a pillow to show him. "Would it help to punch one of these? You could draw or write whatever you want on it."

"Maybe." Min picked one, took it to the checkout, and paid the dollar plus tax.

When we got into the car, I urged, "Try it out. Give it all ya got!"

Min clenched his teeth, held the angry-pillow in one hand, and landed punches with the other. "It works! Hmm. I'll think about what I want to write on it."

Our son needed time to deal with his emotions, but he finally realized God would help him—whatever happened.

You, Goodness and Mercy, are Min's companions. And the angry-pillow? A buck well spent!

You accompany us along this tear-soaked path. Thank you for helping us embrace the Savior and for showing us, without a doubt, we're not alone in this storm.

> Facing another day,
> a family walking an unknown path

FYI:

(kk) Referencing Psalm 23 and Isaiah 40:11

| 26 |

A Change of Heart

"The Lord has ... a plan for my good ...
He knows every option and every possible outcome ...
and always chooses the best." —Deborah Barbee Kessler
(adoptive parent, former cancer patient) [11]

The next day was way different than any other day. Yesterday I heard bad news at my appointments—I had two brain tumors. They couldn't take them all out, and I would have chemotherapy in the future. This didn't faze me right away.

When the awful news hit me, I was horrified and viciously angry! I felt like I had no reason to live. I didn't cry, but I didn't eat breakfast either. Instead, I played a World War II game on my PlayStation 2 and took my anger out on the Nazis, destroyed their leaders, and eliminated them from existence. I captured their jet and flew out of the combat zone with my flying buddies on both sides.

After a while Mom called and asked if I wanted to run errands with her.

I did. I bought a pillow at the thrift store. My plan? Punch it, choke it, throw it, and beat the living daylights out of it—like wrestlers defeating their opponents and like I killed the Nazis.

We got Chinese food for lunch. After fighting Nazis and trying out the pillow, it tasted like victory and settled my anger. Grandma thought Chinese was a good choice, but she hadn't slain any enemies that morning, that I know of.

After lunch, I asked to be excused.

Dad said, "You may, but we'll call you back later for a family meeting."

I cleared my dishes, went upstairs, and played a little.

Then Dad called me down.

I passed Grandma's room and waved, but she didn't wave back because she read after lunch with her eyes closed.

Dad was in his recliner. Mom was on the couch which was different. Usually, I gave a little wave then joked about taking their comfy chairs, and they joked about giving me a knuckle-sandwich. Mom said I could sit in her chair, so I did and crisscrossed my legs.

Dad said, "Yesterday we learned you have two choices about what happens next. Did you understand what the doctors talked about?"

"I have two tumors in my head?"

Dad answered, "Yes. The little one we already knew about. The other one's bigger and deep in your brain."

"Like the small grapefruit one I had in my belly?"

"Not as big as that." Dad turned to Mom and with shaky voice asked, "Can you take it from here?"

Mom nodded then looked my way. "We have a decision to make, but you need to help because this is about you."

"I'm ready. I'll listen." I fiddled with my feet. I had socks on and didn't like sock stuff between my toes, so I pulled them off. Not my toes. The socks.

"One choice is ..."

I put up my pointer finger like number one.

"... to have a biopsy only."

I moved my number-one finger to my cheek to think.

Mom continued, "That means the surgeon goes in and takes little samples out to study so they know what kind of tumor it is and how to treat it."

"Okay. I understand."

"The second choice ..."

I put up two fingers.

"... is to have a small part of the tumor removed."

"Why can't they just take them out—like when I had my belly surgery?"

"The surgeon said they can't. It's got something to do with crossing from one side of your brain to the other."

My fingers dropped down, and I stopped the toe-business. I was lost for words.

"That's the best I can explain right now." Mom's eyes filled with tears. "I absolutely hate NF!" Her tears let go.

Then mine did too. I lowered my head.

Mom came over and put her arm around me.

"This is a very tough situation," Dad said. "We'll help you decide, but we need to make sure we understand what you want."

Mom sat down again.

I put my socks back on and uncrossed my legs. "I think biopsy since they can't take it all out anyway. I don't like talking about this."

"None of us do. We can talk more another time," Dad said.

"Are we done?"

"Sure," Dad added, "but let's pray first." So we did.

I left the room, headed down the hallway, and punched the wall. Then I went upstairs, grabbed the stupid angry-pillow and threw it. And sat-sat-sat until my anger cooled.

Later I asked more questions. How bad was all this? What would happen to me with my choices? My parents had questions too, so they read all the papers the surgeon gave us.

If I chose biopsy, a little patch of hair would be shaved off, the neurosurgeon would cut a door-flap in my scalp-skin, drill a tiny hole through my skull, and take three samples from the tumor.

I thought, with a drilled hole in my head, there would be bloody brains gushing out when I woke up from surgery. This horrified me to an extreme extent, but the doctor said the bone grows back over the hole.

I would stay in the hospital one night. I could order a cheeseburger, fries, soda, and then go home. I wanted to be with my family because everyone was coming to our house for a Thanksgiving feast. Stephen and his wife from Colorado too!

My other choice? Remove part of the big tumor. This was more extreme and meant staying in the hospital more days. I would get more free food, but I might be too miserable to enjoy it. *I was in the hospital that long for my belly surgery. Hmm, I already did that.*

Two choices. Neither one got rid of the cancer. I had to live with that. My small brainstem tumor couldn't be biopsied or taken out. I was stuck with that one, and I stuck with my decision. Biopsy.

My parent said I made a good, hard decision.

A hard-knock choice my parents made was for me to leave the workplace. I was sick, falling, and sent home a lot. I would have brain surgery and another surgery to put in a medical port for chemotherapy. It would be difficult to work in this heartbreaking time.

I was very sad about my downhill life, but Joe the boss understood and invited me to the Christmas party. *I would love that.* Joe gave me some hope.

I wished I didn't have brain cancer or need to make any decision. I just wanted to do all the things a kid out of high school and working does. *Why is this happening to me?*

This happened from my neurofibromatosis type 1. Then I thought about my birth mother. Did she have NF1, same as me? She could have brain tumors too. Was she sick like I was? Did she die? If she did, I wanted to be with her in Heaven. I needed to know! If she was alive, I wanted to find her.

But what if she died without Jesus in her life? Then I would never see her no matter what. I started praying for her and my birth father too. Then, after years of hatred toward them, my anger subsided. My faith in the Lord and praying changed my spirit. I went from a Hyde to a Jekyll inside myself, and the potion was my anger, which was now destroyed.

Dear Birth Father,

I forgive you for leaving me and my mother. It's not like you were the first. There have been a lot of birth fathers who left. Maybe you left because you were afraid. Maybe your parents said no, you couldn't marry my birth mother. Maybe you were ostracized because you got a woman pregnant. I need to let my anger go because holding grudges will just make it worse.

Sincerely,

your son by birth

Dear Birth Mother,

I have more feelings towards you. The day you gave birth to me should have been wonderful for both of us, but it was sad because I couldn't stay with you. You did what you thought was best by signing me to international adoption. You knew I had the best chance at finding a family that way. I wanted a wonderful life with you, but instead, I had a good life in foster care and beyond. Don't worry. My life ended up good.

I have no grudges against you. I think it was hard for you to send me away. You did what you had to do, and I don't hate you for that. I love you, and I hope I can see you again if that is our destiny.

I don't know if you're alive or passed away. I just hope God has touched your soul and helped you so one day we can be reunited in Heaven. I'll be heartbroken if you went to hell. If you have accepted Jesus as your Lord and Savior, then one day we will meet on the other side. But I hope you're still alive.

Sincerely,

your birth son

I don't remember when I understood I was going to die, but somehow it clicked in my broken brain I wouldn't live long. Everyone dies, but not everyone dies this young. I asked God if I could live to be very old, like thirty. That was a long time away, so it sounded good if He said yes.

My parents said it was fine to ask God that. They also said all this would be very hard to talk about, but it was better to talk and get used to it, like regular stuff. Sort of like "Do I need a jacket today?" or "I drew a new Scooby-Doo monster." or "Can I be buried with a Chinese take-out menu?"

I watched lots of videos to forget what was happening. I also drew more Scooby-Doo monsters. One was Headless Lumberjack. He wielded his chainsaw, taking off his own head by accident. A person was tucked inside his coat, so Headless Lumberjack really had a head. I thought *If I don't have a head, my cancer will be gone.*

Not having a head wasn't an option, so I made other plans. In my head, which I still had, I felt like overdosing on medicines. But what if that failed? How would I explain that?

My other option? Use a belt and hang myself, but I couldn't figure what was strong enough upstairs to support my weight. I was a tubby person, would end up on the floor, and "thud!" My parents would yell, "Are you all right?" If I didn't answer, they would come up and rescue me. So that wouldn't work either. I was out of options.

Then many people heard about my difficult situation and wanted to help. People prayed.

Someone sent money for me to go to the aquarium. Another person gave a gift certificate for the Chinese buffet. A package arrived with a Scooby-Doo pillow and blanket. And a lady sent glow-in-the-dark planets and stars to comfort me at night.

There was lots of mail. I kept every bit. These things helped me feel better because I felt loved. All this support gave me a purpose for living.

I was facing impossible odds, but God would go with me. I knew He would do what was best because He proved it numerous times. I had no reason to doubt Him. Just like Karen who had cancer in the Adventures in Odyssey episode. Now I was facing the same thing.

Dad called AIAA (American-side adoption agency). Mrs. Fox, the boss who met Dad in 1996 at SWS hospital (Korean-side adoption agency), still worked there. Dad told her we needed to let Mrs. Choi, my omma, know about my illness; and we would write her a letter.

Mrs. Fox said, "I'm going to South Korea next week. If you mail the letter here, I'll bring it to Mrs. Choi personally. She shouldn't be alone when she gets this news."

So, my parents wrote and mailed it to Mrs. Fox who took it on the plane to the mother of my heart.

Dear Mrs. Choi,   *October 29th, 2013*

This note comes to you to let you know about your beloved Min Soo. You loved him and prayed with him his first 3 years. Then, when God answered your prayer that Min Soo would have a family, it became our privilege to raise him as our son.

Min Soo has brought great joy to our family ... and he has always been blessed and surrounded by people who loved him greatly. He truly won the hearts and love of them all.

This month we learned he has a large, growing tumor in his brain. The doctor tells us the bad news—they cannot take out that tumor or another that is also there.

We thought we could not breathe when the doctor told us, and we are filled with sadness and tears flow much. We think, "How can we enjoy life without our son?" Yet Min Soo loves Jesus as his Savior, and we know he'll be in such a wonderful place, have no more illness or pain, and be with God!

Min Soo is such a brave young man. Dear baby farmer, (mm) *you planted good seeds in his heart, and we've tried to water those. He loves people and understands their hurts, he is funny and helps people laugh ...*

Min Soo is sending gifts ... He picked the bracelet and lamb for you ... and most importantly, Min Soo wanted you to see what a handsome young man he is now! (nn)

We're grateful to God for each day He has lent Min Soo to us. We're also grateful to you for being the first person to teach him what love is and share your family with him. We will keep you in prayer as you grieve this news. When our hearts are heavy, we will know yours are also; and this love and pain will join our hearts across the ocean.

Devotedly,

Brian and Sarah Hampshire

(Min Soo's American family)

FYI:

(ll) Beloved saint and friend—6/13/2019 Facebook excerpt; used with permission

(mm) Mrs. Choi's son's translation of "foster mother" from her letters

(nn) Min's photo—autumn 2013

| 27 |

A Medal of Honor

"He loves me too well to forsake me, or give me
a trial too much ..." —Charles D. Tillman [59]

We woke up when it was still dark and drove to my random hospital. I couldn't eat or drink—just a little water to take my blood pressure pills. I asked all sorts of questions and jabbered the whole way.

My new Scooby-Doo pillow and blanket went with me. Scooby didn't mind because dogs like riding in the car. My parents would make sure he behaved while I was put under.

I don't remember much except telling jokes—no singing in German this time—because I was terrified. I was there to get a brain biopsy and go home the next day.

When I woke up and left recovery, I was wheeled to a room. They moved me from the gurney to the hospital bed. The nurse fixed a bed pad that was folded up around me. *Why is that there?*

My parents came in. That's when I found out someone tripped over my Foley catheter tube when I was asleep before surgery. It ripped out and tore a part inside me I don't want to talk about. It looked like something from a horror movie by the amount of blood, but this was my reality.

That night Mom stayed with me.

The night nurse came in, checked my stats, and lifted back the bed pad to change it. I freaked and was horrified seeing a big puddle of blood! I was positive I was bleeding to death! I begged the nurse to wake up Mom, and he did. She helped me cope.

Sadly, I couldn't go home the next day, but I could order whatever I wanted to eat.

One more sleep and I went home, but I was embarrassed. The catheter was still in me, and a urine bag was tied to my leg. Then I saw my two-times fourth-grade teacher in our house, and I was so happy.

She and her husband drove a long way, and they gave me a Christmas memorabilia—mini-Scooby-Doo lunchbox and thermos. Michael and his wife were there too.

This was a good day.

Dad cared for my biopsy site every day. There was no covering on it. I needed to be careful not to touch it because my busy hands wanted to.

"What does it look like?" I asked Dad when he cleaned it the next time.

"A capital 'L'," Dad answered.

I made an "L" with my fingers and showed Dad. "Like that?"

"Smaller."

"Are there eyes back there?"

Dad laughed.

So, I imagined what was back there. I thought it would go away, but it never will.

But everything I wished came true. I wanted to live until Christmas, and the good news was the tumor was a slower-growing kind and lower stage. I was home before Thanksgiving, and Stephen and his wife were coming soon. Everything was fine except the stupid catheter and bag business. But before Thanksgiving, that became history. I was supremely glad!

Dear Thanksgiving,   *November 2013*

The week before you, we started for the hospital before sunrise, attempting to lighten the mood for totally-wired Min.

Our son was taken to surgery on schedule, but hours stretched beyond what we'd been told.

Finally, we were called. The initial biopsy showed the mass was a juvenile pilocytic astrocytoma—lower stage than originally thought and less aggressive than the adult form. We breathed a sigh of relief, followed by "thank God!"

But all wasn't well. An accident took place involving our son's indwelling catheter, causing a great deal of bleeding and damage to his urethra. How could this happen!

When Min reached step-down ICU, Brian and I were shown to his room. There we explained to Min, best we could, what happened. We weren't sure how much sunk in. He seemed more interested in getting supper. We placed his order.

As Min awaited his meal, Brian readied for home to relieve his mom's 'sitter.

Just then Min's genetics doctor and the department organizer arrived.

Until this fall, we'd always felt they were "medical family." Not now! They hadn't ordered necessary scans and dismissed the 2008 and 2011 MRI results from other hospitals, allowing the mass to become inoperable.

Now they show up? The department organizer said they wanted to see their Min, as she put it. Brian shook his head and made his exit. I wanted to follow.

Min talked with them, mostly about his choice of supper. At that moment he lacked inhibition, tore back his bedding, and folded down the blood-filled pad diapering him.

The genetics doctor gagged and beelined toward the door. He stopped, took some deep breaths, and returned but not within Min's view.

I was shocked at what Min did yet glad he upset the doctor. I thought—
serves you right! I wish you'd leave! Instead, I told our son to cover himself.

Then they left.

After evening rounds, we turned in, leaving on one dim light. I was
deep in sleep when the nurse awoke me.

"Your son's distressed."

I went to Min's bedside. I'd never seen so much blood and also wanted
to gag and turn away, but I needed to distract Min while the nurse finished
cleaning him.

I asked him if he thought Chuck Norris would make another TV
series. Did he have new ideas for Scooby monsters? What was the topic of his
latest list? I rambled on till the mess was cleaned up and Min settled. Then I
explained he must stay in the hospital until the bleeding stopped.

Brian returned in the morning, and I headed home.

The next day Brian called. "The bleeding's nearly controlled, so I'll stay
put. I'm pushing to get Min released, but he'll come home with a catheter and
bag and need follow up to see if there's permanent damage."

Min came home the Saturday before you, Thanksgiving. Church ladies
provided a meal, which we shared with company. An embarrassed Min walked
like a cowboy who'd been on his horse too long, but he enjoyed his guests.

More packages arrived—one from Mrs. Choi, his omma with her words:

"I always thought Min Soo is a special child, but to know that
Min Soo has been going through such pain tears my heart apart ...
God, please let Min Soo carry no burdens on his shoulders, let him not
know what pain is and also let him know that meeting and parting
opens another new way of life. God, please walk with Min Soo and let
him know that he isn't alone. I would like to give this hat (PP) to Min

Soo ... to become a person that could say that 'everything is so warm and beautiful.' From Min Soo's foster mother in Seoul."

A large envelope arrived from Chuck Norris! ("How far away is Texas?" Min asked each time we moved to see if we were getting closer.) Enclosed was an 8 x 10 autographed photo along with a handwritten note on embossed stationery:

"Dear Min,

I was told about your condition. I am very sorry to hear about it and I will be praying that a miracle will happen. Min, miracles happen all the time, so why not with you. If not, then I will meet you in heaven and I will give you a few Martial Art lessons. I plan on teaching up there. Min, you take care my friend ...

Always a friend,

(signed) Chuck Norris"

Before Min's biopsy, mail poured in and now continued—two bank-file boxes full of cards, letters, school children's drawings, and numerous gifts.

"I can't believe this many people care about me," our son expressed.

A handmade quilted throw with Bible verses from a church women's group arrived. Min covered himself with it. "Those are good verses for when I can't sleep." Then a hand-drawn poster from an author/cartoonist (oo)added a dream. "If I keep practicing, maybe someday I'll draw that good."

A couple, whose daughter had brain cancer, started a charity for kids with the same. They "adopted" Min and sent numerous food, gas, and retail gift cards. We wept and thanked God for provisions through Kate's family! Her testimony also showed Min a person with brain cancer can still be used of God.

Thanksgiving, you've passed now, and, even though we're still dealing
with raw emotions, we thank God Who showers Min and us with good. May
we remember this as we face an unknown-to-us future.

Exceedingly grateful,
Min's parents

I was sitting on my downstairs bed. (I had one on each level now
so my parents could help me downstairs and upstairs.)

I looked up random My Little Pony images to cheer me and feel
better. Stephen came in and sat on my bed carefully so I wouldn't get
dizzy. His wife joined him. I placed my laptop aside. Stephen reached
into his pocket and pulled out a badge—a special award called a Bronze
Star he was given while serving in the war.

Stephen and his wife presented this to me because he said I was
facing the biggest war of all—my fight against brain cancer and future
chemo battles. He pinned it onto my shirt. It felt nice having an Army
medal, but I didn't understand the full meaning.

Later I took the pin off so it wouldn't go through the washer and
clank like crazy in the dryer. I noticed something on the back—"Min"
engraved on it. I realized then my brother wasn't loaning me his heroic
medal. He made it mine to keep forever. It made me feel special and
gave me courage to move forward.

I looked up "Bronze Star" [qq] on my laptop and read more.
Then it sunk in what this fully meant when my brother did this heart-
warming act.

FYI:

[oo] Ed Vandemark—cartoonist/author

[pp] Warm cap with South Korean Taeguk Warriors "football"
team logo

[qq] Military award for heroic act or meritorious service in a combat
zone

| 28 |

A Memorable Christmas

"A tree with deep roots stands firm in the storm; It bears abundant flowers and fruit." —a Korean proverb [60]

A big package arrived December 7th from some unknown address. I opened it and found traditional clothing of my homeland. Who sent it, and how did this person know the hanbok would give me peace, happiness, and tranquility? A family friend tells about this:

When I found out Min had brain tumors, my heart ached for Brian, Sarah, and their family. I wanted to give Min something very special and meaning-filled. Sarah mentioned wanting to get Min a hanbok. My family decided to do this. She didn't mention seeing one they liked—only that it was my choice.

I searched the Internet and found a beautiful, manly hanbok. The seller sent it directly to Min.

When we chatted again, I told Sarah a hanbok was on its way and included a photo from the ad. We rejoiced seeing the Lord's Hand in this as we'd both chosen the same hanbok."
—Judi

This special-occasion hanbok, honoring my culture, had embroidered ornamentation of silk and silver threads and two brass fasteners reminding me of small, colorful Fabergé eggs.

I became curious and researched the Korean meaning of the ornamentation. Crane: longevity, purity, peace. Deer: long life. Fish: fearlessness, freedom (but the fish was in the crane's mouth, so I don't think it felt those). Clouds: long life. Sun: longevity because "it rises in the sky each day without fail." 61

The hanbok connected me to my families in South Korea—birth and foster. I was proud to own such a treasure and told my parents, "I want to be buried in this."

But my hope boosted upward! Maybe I'll get married like my brothers and wear my hanbok then! But I don't know if there's a wife for me because I'm a child in a man's body.

Dear Abby,   *2013*

Recently our son mentioned the topic of marriage. This isn't, however, the first time.

April Fool's Day his kindergarten year Min joked, "Let's tell my aide I got married!" I wrote in his back-and-forth school notebook, "Please excuse Min next week. He's getting married and will return soon after."

That noon Min smiled, handing me the reply. "Congratulations! Will Min bring his new bride to school? If so, we'll pour an extra juice for snack."

Then this, a decade later during a dental emergency: The dentist ever-so-sweetly comforted Min as she worked. "How's that feel, hon?" and "Let me know if this hurts, hon."

Min lifted his head and turned toward me. "Is she married?"

"Yes," I answered.

"Then what business does she have calling me hon?"

The dentist totally lost it and stepped out to regain her composure.

In all seriousness, though, Min would like a wife, believing this is just how it is because he's witnessed his brothers' marriages. We don't oppose this idea. He does, however, have qualifications.

Min states, "I want an Asian wife with Jesus in her life who isn't indecently exposed."

Of course, if he marries, he and his wife will need supervised living if they both function at about the same level.

Min wonders why he doesn't fit into grown-up life. "I haven't even had a girlfriend. I want to get married and have a kid."

"Could you take care of a child?" I asked.

He folded his arms. "I'd love it and feed it!"

"Could you bathe and dress a baby? Take a baby to doctors' appointments?"

Min's arms dropped to his sides. "My wife could dress it, but someone needs to run the bath water, like you do for me, because I can't tell if it's too hot or too cold, and I don't always remember to turn off the water. I can't take it to the doctor though."

"That's important because any child born to you might have NF1," Brian added.

Min lowered his head. "I don't want my kid to have NF and tumors and get teased." He was quiet a moment. "What if it got cancer?"

"That's a serious consideration. Also, you're not likely to live a long time. How would a wife feel about that?" I asked.

"Sad, unless God takes my tumors away. He can do that."

"He can, but so far He hasn't chosen that for you," Brian added.

"I need to pray about this. Maybe I could just have a good friend who's a girl. If only girls didn't make me so nervous!"

Well, Abby, problem solved for now, but the subject will likely surface again.

> *Guiding the bachelor,*
> *his counselors*

When I dropped out of the workplace, Joe invited me back for the Christmas party. I wanted to give gifts, so we prepared a basket of small things.

When Joe saw me, he heart-warming hugged me—like friends who hadn't seen each other for a long while. Reuniting felt like peace.

The employees were excited to see me! They had an assortment of food and beverages, and then they gave gifts. I wasn't expecting anything because I didn't work there anymore, but they gave me a DVD player. I was outstanded by this!

Now I missed being part of the group more, but I would be a risk with chemo starting soon and immune-compromised. I told my parents I missed the workplace and getting paid. Even though they employed me at home now, I still wanted to earn more money.

Mom had an idea. "How 'bout we give you hard-knock pay for chemo? That'll definitely be hard work."

I put my thumb and pointer finger across my chin. "Hmm. That's a good plan!"

Another nice thing happened! When Kate (a girl with brain cancer) and her family sent us many gift cards, there was one for Toys-R-Us! I couldn't wait to use that! They also sent a photo of Kate. I kept it to remember to pray for her.

We had to go to the hospital to get my stitches out. That meant passing Toys-R-Us. But first the stitch-business. My dark, thick

Korean hair grew fast—like a male Rapunzel—making this a challenge, but the doctor got them all.

Toys-R-Us next! Now I could buy some Ponies! I picked an assortment of blind-bag My Little Ponies and Scooby-Doo DVDs. I felt grown-up paying with my own gift card—all thanks to "Kate's Crazy Cool Christmas!"

Shot Glass: *New Year's Day 2014*

Never did I expect to find one of you in our home! As I gathered Min's Christmas decorations to pack away, though, there you were—set before little Lord Jesus lying in the manger.

I glared at Min. "What in the world are you doing with this? And why is it in your nativity scene?"

Min looked at me sheepishly. "I got it from the prize machine at the bowling alley."

"Do you know what this is?"

"A cup?"

"Yeah! For alcoholic drinks!"

Min lowered his head and teared up. "Sorry. I thought it was one of those cups like we use at church."

Then I lowered my head. "Oh, Min. I'm so sorry."

Humbled by our son's act of worship—presenting his "myrrh" before the Christ Child, I saw that, through his eyes, you were a most fitting gift and right where you belonged.

"O come, let us adore Him." [62]

> *On bended knee,*
> *one of His sheep*

| 29 |

Frenemy

*"While your story may be filled with unbelievable
hurt or disappointment, I still believe
you're right where you belong."*
—*Trisha White Priebe* (adoptee, adoptive parent) [63]

My brain mass grew little bits between September 2013 and January 2014.

In February, I had surgery to put in the medical port. Dad took me because Mom caught pneumonia after Christmas—not the contagious kind, but she was sick a long time.

I was horrified about being put to sleep because of the bloody-bag incident, but my surgeon and Dad assured me I would have no catheter for this short surgery. The medi-port went into my upper left chest under my skin. I stayed overnight. Dad did too. I ordered my usual dinner.

The next morning, I had my first chemo treatment. Dr. Choo, my oncologist, said with this kind of chemo, I wouldn't lose my hair. They numbed the port area with a thick special cream we used every time one-half-hour before chemo started. Then a big needle was inserted through my skin and the medi-port, and bags of wash and chemical dripped into me for six hours. That stuff made a bitter, metalish taste in my mouth.

The nurses made sure I had medicines for nausea and vomiting and special mouthwash to help with sores. I was on steroids around chemo time and another medicine in case I broke out in hives.

Then we went home.

The first week I heaved like a ginormous cat coughing up a furball. It felt like all my insides came out. I kneeled on the bathroom floor, leaning over the toilet with my eyes closed so I wouldn't see what ran out my mouth and nose. My throat burned. Mom sat on the edge of the tub by me and rubbed my back.

I took a deep breath between heaves and told Mom, "You don't have to be here. I don't want you to get more sick."

"You're not contagious," Mom replied, "and I can stand it."

"I just thought you don't want to see this."

Mom stopped rubbing but kept her hand on my back. "I wish I could take this from you. I'd rather it was me with cancer."

I heaved again, grabbed some toilet paper, and wiped my mouth and nose. I took another breath and looked at Mom. "But then I would lose another mother." I started to cry.

Mom cried too.

Every Tuesday I had blood drawn to check that my cell counts were a safe level. After the very first blood draw, they dived super low. I ran a fever and stayed in my safety bubble, which was my home, until the next morning when I needed transfusion.

I had to go perfectly clean and be gowned in sterile garb. Everyone who entered the room had to do that too. It took a few hours, then we headed home, but we couldn't eat out or get take-out.

My birthday arrived—twenty-one! I made it to adult age! My parents let me pick a special place to eat. I chose Red Lobster. Almost all my family met us there—Stephen too who moved here from Colorado.

After Thanksgiving the year before, when they went home, Stephen's wife said, "We need to be closer to your family. They need us." This was a huge deal! She sacrificed being near her family to move across the country to be with us.

Stephen was emotionally happy by his wife's warm-hearted act. They put their house for sale, and Stephen came ahead to get a place to live then came to my party.

In the parking lot, Stephen passed off a gift to me—like a hot potato—a stuffed musician Pony named Octavia. He was embarrassed, but I cherished it. I clutched it just like my bag of little cars when I came to America.

When my blood was okay and I could shop, I bought more blind-bag Ponies and got many duplicates. *What am I going to do with these?* The Ponies said (squeaky-like because they were small, and tiny things talk that way), "Give us to other people!" *Great idea,* so we did a bro fist-bump—my fist-to-their-hooves agreement.

La-la-lolly-dah! Time for chemo again. I brought Ponies for the nurses. They loved them, compared Ponies, and straddled them on their stethoscopes. This boosted them during long days. For me? It spread friendship, which the Ponies teach, and gave me joy.

Dr. Choo came on rounds. A nurse asked him, "Did you get a Pony?"

He lowered his head. "No. I am not Pony-worthy."

I dug in my backpack and found a Dr. Hooves Pony. It was my favorite. I didn't have another one. But they were both doctors, so I gave mine to Dr. Choo.

He smiled.

By now I saved enough money from working, graduation, and chemo to buy a bike, but a two-wheel bike wasn't possible. I was in bad shape. My only option? A three-wheel one and wear a helmet. I didn't want to. Besides where would we find a helmet for my bigger-than-normal head? But Mom found one, so I was stuck.

There was a nice three-wheel adult bike with a big rear basket for sale. We bought it, but I never got good riding this bike. It wasn't like before. No wind blew in my face unless it was windy because I couldn't go fast. Mostly the bike sat in the garage keeping the spiders company.

I really wanted another two-wheel bike. I hoped to be well enough for that someday.

Chemo was a nightmare—enduring extreme sickness (even with pills to help), every-week blood draws, low blood counts, dizziness and falling. We bought a wheelchair at the thrift store so I could navigate in the outside world. I used an electric cart at stores.

I slept tons. Every activity exhausted me. So did puking. Sometimes, I laid on the bathroom floor (downstairs during the day), too tired to move. But I had to, or Grandma would trip over me because of her poor eyesight.

Before chemo started, I visited Grandma in her room and had good talks. Little kitty was excited to see me, and I petted it. But after chemo started, I was too sick and had no energy.

After Grandma learned about my brain cancer, one day at the table she said, "I know Min is going to be healed. Everything will be okay."

I was busy eating and didn't say anything.

Dad waited until we finished and I was excused.

I walked to my downstairs area and clicked away on my laptop, but I could hear the conversation.

"Mom, please don't say that in front of Min."

Grandma raised her voice, "But I know he'll be healed. We just need enough faith."

"God heals. We firmly believe that, but it's not the amount of faith. It's Who you put your faith in," Dad said, "Min will be healed either here or in Heaven. We're praying God's will be done. What you're saying will upset Min if God chooses not to heal him on earth."

Grandma wasn't happy. I could tell, and I never heard her argue before. She loved me, but what she said confused me because my tumors were still growing.

When Jesus was on earth. He healed disabled and sick people. I wanted God to heal me, but He didn't heal everyone here because He had other assignments. He turned some people down because He needed to spread the Word of God.

God never took away my disability, but I never asked Him. I wouldn't know until the next MRI if my tumors were gone. I said to the technician then, "I think my tumors are gone because I asked God to take them away." But they weren't.

In May 2014 we sold our house and would move closer to my brothers. Grandma said she wasn't moving with us because she would die soon. My ninety-eight-year-old grandma was diagnosed with cancer too. My parents had full hands.

One morning I was coming downstairs and tumbled downward. Grandma came by with her walker and started to fall too. Mom quick-as-a-flash looked at me and let me fall and caught Grandma instead.

I looked at Mom in a questioning manner. *Why didn't Mom help me?* Later she told me this super-fast decision broke her heart, but Grandma could break bones and need to go to the hospital if she chose me. Mom said it very hurt making this choice.

Before Grandma passed, she told me little kitty would become mine. I was familiar with adoption.

My grandma died. Dad went to the funeral. I couldn't go because me and Mom had to be at stupid chemo. I was very sad about that.

We stopped a couple times for me to vomit, so Mom let me buy soda even though it was early morning. I needed my wheelchair to navigate from the parking garage to chemo. Mom leaned on it because she was still weak.

I told the nurses about Grandma passing. They extra comforted me.

At chemo I could get vending machine snacks and order lunch.

To Carboplatin: *February through August 2014*

Years ago, we owned a poster with a doughy-looking cartoon character named Ziggy [64] *standing between two boulders—the left chiseled with "rock" and the right, "hard place." You're the embodiment of that poster's message.*

How can we express what it felt like, reading about you? Although you shrink or stabilize brain cancer, you can cause hearing loss, intoxicate the vestibular system, damage kidneys, and in time cause blood/bone cancer.

We reviewed Min's MRI reports. With the mass still growing, there we were, subbing for Ziggy between those boulders. But knowing our son wanted to "live to be really old—like thirty," we signed consent.

Min would have chemo monthly for one year with blood draws weekly to check cell counts. Every third month: Kidney function test with injected dye, hearing test, and an additional MRI on two different days than chemo.

Month one: Min struggled with many side effects. Also, cell counts plunged, and he needed transfusion.

We tried to encourage Min, telling him hundreds of people were praying.

"Are a million people praying for me?"

His dad smiled. "No, but maybe a thousand. People all around the world are praying."

"Is anyone in Thailand praying for me?" Min asked, remembering he prayed for a little Thai boy adopted by a Christian couple we learned about.

Brian caught on. "Could be."

Month two: 5:00 a.m. departure for 6:30 a.m. chemo. I was weak but able to take Min.

Month three: Brian's turn to take Min. First Tuesday afterward his counts dropped. Confined to home!

Month four: More pressure from the boulders! Min's grandma lay dying. She couldn't speak but pressed little kitty to her lips as Min said goodbye. Then he went to bed.

Mom died in the night. I helped the hospice nurse ready her for the mortician with whom Brian spoke previously because he didn't want Min to see her deceased. The mortician came before daylight.

I stripped the bed, sprayed the air, then closed the door.

When Min awoke, he noticed the closed door and knew she passed. He went into her room, and I followed. Min walked over and picked up the little stuffed kitten. "I'll take good care of little kitty for Grandma."

Tuesday Brian left for the funeral in New York. I took Min to chemo. We both ached to be with Brian.

We opted to leave our bedroom upstairs to keep Min company. Our rooms shared a wall, and Min knocked on it when he needed help. He struggled getting out of bed and fell walking to the bathroom. We padded the way.

One evening after we already bedded down, Min knocked on our door. "Can I come in and give you hugs?" He rarely showed affection.

"Sure," Brian replied.

Min came in, waved like he always did, then hugged us both. He left, and we turned off the lights.

A short time later he knocked again. "Can I come in and give you hugs?"

"You already hugged us goodnight," we answered, thinking he'd forgotten.

"That wasn't your goodnight hugs. That was your I'm-glad-I'm-your-son hugs." Round two.

Month five: Those boulders! Min's counts plunged into the danger zone. We sent out an urgent prayer request as we were amidst a move. God answered. Min recovered without transfusion.

Min's half-way-through-chemo MRI result: No change. Our hearts sank.

Dr. Choo encouraged us though. "We hoped the tumors would shrink, but they've not grown. This is a partially good result." He also said this type of tumor can sleep.

"You mean Min won't die any time soon?" I asked.

"A tumor may sleep five or ten years. Sometimes longer. When it awakens and grows, another chemotherapy regimen may arrest it. This can happen repeatedly until it 'spiders.'"

Hope! Extended time!

Ziggy stood between that "rock" and a "hard place." So have we. Yet, we learned it wasn't an impossible place when leaning on the Rock of Ages.

Min called chemo both "friend" and "enemy!" Maybe we'll rename the boulders!

> *Guardedly yet gratefully,*
> *Min's parents*

We moved on July 4th. The new city welcomed us with fireworks! I would like living near my brothers, their wives, and kids because the family grew exponentially. (Nathan and his wife later had a son they named after me!)

Our new location was interesting with various colors of people from around the world. The grocery store had a whole Asian food aisle! We shopped at the Asian market too.

There I wandered the aisles. Then I spotted a breathtaking wall hanging of circle wood, brass with stamped Korean writing, and long tassels. I grabbed it and hurried to Mom. "Can we please buy this?"

Mom was outstanded by it. "Sure! For your new room."

I rushed to the checkout and asked if the man was Korean, but I was speaking Tasmanian Devil-speed. He couldn't understand me. I reminded myself, *Speak—slowly—and— clearly!* "Can—you—translate—this?"

He said, "This say treat like you want treated."

Mom said, "Oh, the Golden Rule!" [rr]

My mind lit up. "That's like the Ponies teach."

Mom looked at me weird-like. "This is a Bible verse, Min."

Then I wanted it even more. I bought it and hung it in my room, and it felt like a piece of my homeland was with me.

FYI:

(rr) Referencing Luke 6:31

| 30 |

Through Time and Space

"Whatever my lot, Thou hast taught me to say, It is well, it is well with my soul." —Horatio G. Spafford [65]

Since we lived further from my random hospital now and had appointments over two days, we slept in a motel.

Day One: My six-month MRI.

Done.

Then we picked up this kid and took him shopping and out to eat. Jason always called me "Pappy." I don't know why. Maybe I was a father-figure to him. He was more hyperactive than me and talked-talked-talked. I loved when he visited and when he went home because I was exhausted.

One time, Jason slept over and snuck upstairs. I was sitting at my desk. He screamed, "Boo!" I clenched my fists, ready to defend myself. My sensory deprivation scrambled my emotions. I feared this happening again, so I wouldn't let my parents move my desk if it obstructed the view from my door.

Other than that, Jason was cool. We knew him because Dad led him to the Lord at Kentucky Speedway. They formed a lasting bond, and we enjoyed Raceway Ministries Family Fun Day together.

Day Two: My last appointment with my oncologist and his nurse.

Dr. Choo told us my tumors didn't shrink. This saddened me, but he said no growth might mean my tumors could be sleeping.

Time to say goodbye. I gave Dr. Choo Korean art and his nurse a small disco ball. I would miss them. We had five chemos together. Dr. Choo shook my hand and said, "I hope your tumors sleep a long, long time." I hoped that too. Living instead of dying was of great interest to me. My parents agreed.

(My next MRI in three months would show if my tumors really fell asleep.)

I fully thought my tumors were gone, but they weren't. *God loves me. If my tumors aren't gone, He must have a good reason because He knows what He's doing.* I knew He answered people's prayers because He answered many of mine. I still asked God sometimes to remove the cancer, but I left it in His Hands.

I thought more. *I can tell people about Jesus at my new chemo location. If I don't have cancer, I can't do that. This is a monumentous appointment—a mission from God—a job I need to do! This isn't just to get my dose of chemical.*

I still want to live to be really old and have wrinkles, gray hair, and a sensei mustache; but God knows what's best. If I die, it's okay because my cancer will be gone. So will NF1, the mystery genetic problem, and Asperger's. That's a miracle!

After my oncology appointment, we headed to the Creation Museum.

When I had my brain biopsy, the museum staff sent a special photograph greeting they signed. I couldn't believe they wrote, prayed for me, and invited me to be their guest sometime. Now that special day arrived, so we tried to put aside our heart-sadness.

Tom was our tour guide and Dad's friend from Raceway Ministries. He worked at the museum. Tom and his wife always encouraged me with special mail.

We arrived late from my appointment, so I missed meeting Ken Ham, founder of Answers in Genesis,[66] who wanted to greet me. He had to catch a plane but was willing to return. My parents said not to worry about it and thanked him. I was disappointed, but I cheered up when Tom led us to where Buddy Davis [67] gave a concert.

I talked with Buddy about the flaming lizard-effect in his video. This inspired me and cured my disappointment about not meeting Ken Ham. Buddy sang and dedicated a song to me. It was heart-warming and made me happy.

My day was amazing! I loved a special bug exhibit, all the sights, and the food. They took our picture pretending to be terrified of a projected attacking dinosaur.

Tom presented me with a Creation Museum souvenir book. Then we met his wife, and he told her, "This is the fastest tour I ever gave!"

Next, we rode uphill by golf cart to the petting zoo and spotted the animals! I didn't see the "Don't-pick-up-the-chickens!" sign and carried them all over in their pen. I fed them too. And I saw a quagga—part horse and part zebra.

The petting zoo was outstanding! After that, though, I plopped on the ground. I was exhausted, but I had the greatest time of my life. I asked my parents, "Do you think someday I could work here with the animals?"

"Too far. Sorry," Dad said.

I wish I wasn't so far. This would be my dream job since Camp KYSOC closed.

When we got in the car, I said, "This was one of the very best days!" Then I fell asleep.

Chemo six would be at the new cancer center. A nurse showed us around the circle-shaped room. "We have four patients in each pod."

My eyes lit up, and I smiled. "An alien pod!" *Is this a spaceship?* "I'll like it here."

The pods were cubbies with four recliners and half-walls. The nurses' station—or command central, if it was a spaceship—was in the middle of the pods.

Dad took me to Best Buy. I bought a tablet to keep me busy at chemo. I loved this idea.

Chemo six was the next week—shorter here because they used one bag of "wash" instead of two like before—plus the chemical. But there was still enough time to tell my pod-people about God, it's okay whatever happens because I'll go to Heaven, and I'm not afraid.

This place had free snacks and microwave stuff, but they didn't serve meals.

I had chemo seven and eight with no repercussions.

But at chemo nine in October something malfunctionally happened. I was getting my chemical and talking with fellow pod-people. One was a dude my age. We talked about video games and life with cancer. I said I would pray for him. He thanked me and left when his chemicals finished.

I turned on my tablet and played a My Little Pony game.

Suddenly, my feet started to itch. I scratched through my socks then furiously yanked them off and franticly yelled, "My feet itch so badly, but now they're burning too!" It felt like severe carpet burn deep into my feet. They swelled and turned as red as a super-bad sunburn.

Mom was shocked and got my nurse. The nurse quick clamped off my IV. Then she ran to the nurses' station (command central) and picked up the phone (transmitter).

Mom ran to her and asked what was happening!

"It's an allergic reaction. I need to reach the doctor on call."

Mom came back. By then, my hands swelled—like an old Tom and Jerry [68] cartoon where a mouse blew up its hand to make it puffed to sock a cat.

Then my neck swelled too. I cried out but wasn't coherent. I groaned and felt pain like I couldn't describe. Finally, the nurse came with the antidote, and it flowed into me. Eventually I deflated and started feeling better.

At my next oncology appointment, the doctor said my last three chemo sessions were canceled. I couldn't have any more chemo by IV because other drugs would do worse to me.

The good news? No more chemo by IV or weekly blood draws, and my medi-port would be removed. The bad news? My list of future chemo options got shorter—only chemo pills, if my tumors grew again.

I felt happy and relieved. I wanted chemo to live longer, but it was a nightmare of torturous horror. I didn't really think about the bad news.

Dear Olive,   *October 2014*

You incredible dog! Do you remember when we met?

Our son accompanied me to pick up a secondhand headboard. Min was post-chemo with some good days and glad to go out. We found your home and parked in the driveway. Min waited in the car while I went to the door and knocked.

A lady answered with you at her side—you groomed-to-perfection English Sheepdog.

I told her why I'd come and commented how lovely you were. She told me your name was Olive, and you were a cancer dog that helped patients through treatment. I mentioned our son, a cancer patient, was with me. I asked if he could meet you! She agreed, and she'd see us by the garage where the headboard was.

I went to the car. "Min, you'll want to meet this pup!"

Being an animal lover, Min got right out and joined me by the garage door, which hummed upward. There you were at the lady's side. You stood in front of Min. He squatted close to you, and you laid down.

Min's eyes were fixed on you when he asked, "Can I give her a treat?"

"Sure. I'll get one." The lady left. You followed her. She returned shortly, and you laid again in front of our son.

Min offered the treat, but you refused it. He held it so close it touched your mouth. You still refused. "I don't think she likes me." Min stood up, dropping his arms to his sides, still holding the treat.

I saw the disappointment in his eyes. "Maybe she has a tummy ache."

"She's fine," the lady said. "She thinks she's working. She knows she's not supposed to eat when she works."

At that moment, what had already shattered us, devastated again. Olive, you knew.

Your people friend,

Sarah

| 31 |

"Keep Strong!"

"... Be strong and of a good courage; fear not ...
the Lord thy God is with thee whithersoever thou goest."
Joshua 1:9 [69]

No more chemo! I was free but so dizzy, like a wrestler who took a punch to the head and felt suspended in mid-air even though my feet were on the ground. Spooky! I didn't always know when I would fall, so I couldn't stop myself. Dad unpacked Grandma's walker for me.

The day before Thanksgiving, I took a worst turn. I felt like SpongeBob when he had "the suds" [70] and turned a different color from sickness—but worse.

Dad called my oncologist, and the doctor said, "Go to the emergency room." So we went.

The doctor thought my tumors could be growing. I groaned. *More torture.* He ordered an MRI. Dad stayed with our stuff and guarded my tablet while I was wheeled to radiology.

This basement room was tiny. Me and Mom were alone until a man arrived in an orange jumpsuit with his wrists and ankles chained together. An armed guard was with him.

Mom said hello. I managed a slight wave. I didn't know then, but Mom was thinking what to say because "nice weather" and stuff wouldn't do. Then she said to the man, "This time of year must be hard for you. I hope you find God's peace at this Thanksgiving time then have a meaning-filled Christmas too. I'll pray for you both."

They thanked her.

Mom thought the guard wouldn't let her say more, so she stopped.

I said, "I'll pray too."

When the MRI was over, Mom helped me out of the room and into the wheelchair. We returned to the ER. Later results came back, and everything was the same. That made me feel better but not unsick better.

Nathan called Dad and offered to bring meals from our early-planned family Thanksgiving, but we weren't home until dark. We were sad to miss that, but I believe we needed to be in the MRI waiting room to talk to the prisoner and guard.

But Mom felt like she failed by not saying more. Maybe we both did. We said we would pray for them, but after that we forgot. We broke the promise. But why did this re-memory show up? God gave us another chance to pray now. I hope the Holy Spirit sent someone to finish the task.

The next day we became hobbits and had second-Thanksgiving even though we missed the first one. Some of Stephen's wife's family visited. This was a fun day with family and not-family.

And I was well enough to go to church on Sunday.

Dear Pastors whose sermons include rhetorical questions,　　　　*2014*

Warning! If we visit your church, our son may answer your rhetorical questions out loud.

The first time this happened, Min answered a pastor's "Should I not be willing to take up my cross and follow Him?" with "Yes, we all should."

We shushed him.

Min looked our way, shrugged, and said aloud, "Well, he asked!"

We suggest you remove these types of questions because you never know what will come out of that mouth or when. Besides, shouldn't rhetorical questions remain unanswered?

With reddened cheeks,
folks remaining anonymous

I wanted to return to our mountain hometown for the Christmas parade, but I was so sick the week before. We almost canceled plans, but I improved with anti-dizziness medicine from the ER.

I was as excited as a monkey getting bunches of bananas! Not just about seeing the parade, but I was invited to ride in it as grand marshal!

But it rained on parade day, and it was canceled. I was saddened. My big opportunity gone, but I could still visit friends because my family and the town planned an open house.

That was fun, and the food was delicious. There were even Doritos, which bonded me to Blake who shared hers with me in school years before. She made creative welcome signs. (I kept them.) Other friends came, and one wrote:

"Min is the kindest, gentlest, and most true soul I have ever had the pleasure of calling my friend. He faces his adversities with unshakeable faith and outpourings of love ... He is the embodiment of grace.

I will never understand why bad things happen to good people. Min's situation makes that realization seem all the more heavy. Burdened with the unimaginable weight of cancer, Min still shines. Min makes my heart sing. His smiles are still feather light and that humbles me beyond all measure.

You restore my hope, Min. I am awed by your courage and beauty."—Jess

My school teachers, aide, missionary friends, and classmates came. Mrs. Martha too! She was hefty old—not fat—just struggling because she was sick. She said, "I wouldn't have missed this for the world!" Mrs. Martha inspired me because her faith in God was strong. She mentor-tutored me out of her heart's goodness.

When all the town's police and fire department vehicles showed up, I was super surprised! "Is this all for me?" A fireman signaled for me to come, and I climbed into the cab with Santa. Dad, Stephen, and two little nephews joined the parade too.

We rode throughout the town with sirens and flashing lights, and the fire chief let me blow the horn. I did "dum-duhduh-dum-dum" ... and the firetruck behind us replied, "dum-dum." I smiled so big! I felt like king of the world, which was a big promotion from canceled grand marshal.

Back at the community room/library, I couldn't believe my eyes! The local news [71] came with a camera, reporter, and microphone. They wanted me to say something.

I thought super-fast. A news story grieved me about a woman with brain cancer who wanted to be killed by doctor-assisted suicide. The court obliged her.

I'm now the age she was when this happened and imagine how fearful her thoughts were about going through horrible suffering. Maybe this caused her to take this action to stop the pain.

At the time the woman did this I was twenty-one with brain cancer, and I asked a lot of questions. Inside me was a battle between good and evil. Good said live, stay strong, and fulfill your purpose. God will be with you always and forever. Evil said ending it is the best option. You're going to a good place anyway, and you feel lousy and miserable, like a Zombie.

I asked my parents, "When the time comes, if I'm in so much pain, will you help me die like that lady?"

"No. We can't do that, but we'll help you through it."

"How?"

"There's a super strong medicine that kills pain, and we'll give you that and make sure you're as comfortable as possible."

There were other talks with my parents because I thought about the inevitable. I had that large mass deep in my brain. I also had that size-of-a-blueberry tumor over 1 cm. The midbrain is 2 cm. and getting clogged.

My brainstem "regulates heart rate, breathing, balance, coordination, reflexes." [72] The midbrain "affects vision, hearing, motor-control, sleep and wakefulness, alertness, temperature regulation." [73] So, this blueberry-sized tumor is an apocalyptic nightmare!

I didn't want to deal with all this. I understood why the woman wanted to ease her pain, but the way she was doing it was wrong.

The next news article said she died. I was devastated. *What if she didn't know Jesus? Then she was doomed to a worser fate. What if doctors found a cure soon? It's too late for her.*

When the news interviewed me, this came from my thoughts:

"Before I was really mad about my brain cancer, but now I'm calm. I want to say something to all those people out there right now: Never give up! Keep strong!"

A newspaper reporter also quoted my teacher who repeated fourth grade.

"Min is an inspiration to those he's around. Sometimes I think he taught me the most. I've learned the importance and joy of working with students who have special needs, and more recently I've learned from him about inner strength and un-selfishness.

It's such an honor to know Min. If everyone had his positive attitude, the world would be a better place."

—Mrs. Breeding [74]

I was touched in my heart by her words. My teacher also said that you don't often hear of someone who wants to visit their small town and school.

But for me? I just wanted to be home again.

Bucket List,   *December 2014*

You're getting shorter—bringing both joy and sorrow. May I explain by introducing Min's favorite "Touched by an Angel" episode? [75]

Petey, a terminally ill boy, makes one of you, Bucket List. One wish involves his mom finishing a song she began when he was born. She completes it and sings "Testify to Love" [76] *while Petey listens, then passes. A flag with "Petey is here!" is raised at the end so the angels can find him.*

Min wants mini-flags on his pencils as remembrances with "Min was here!" because "God knows where I am." This idea noted. Check! He asked his dad to prerecord "Testify to Love" for his funeral. Check!

Min openly talked about his inoperable cancer at church and how he hoped to do special things—like Petey. People didn't know who Petey was, but they realized Min was describing you, Bucket List—a term unfamiliar to him.

The church collected enough funds to grant three of Min's wishes. What an outpouring of love!

First, a countryside train ride! Min enjoyed the rhythmic clickity-clacks until the gentle sways made him ill, but he expressed joy about the journey to nowhere and back.

Then a riverboat dining cruise for four (our niece was visiting)! A DJ provided music and welcomed special requests.

I went with our niece to ask for a favorite song, and—with her help locating it on her phone—the DJ patched it into his system.

Back at our table, Min pushed his dinner aside—the motions making him queasy. He lay his head on folded arms and closed his eyes.

Just then the DJ announced, "Min Hampshire, here's one for you!"

Min opened his bloodshot eyes—a sign his equilibrium was challenged—and commented with awe, "He said my name," then closed his eyes again.

"Testify to Love" filled the room. Min didn't move but smiled. When the song ended, his cousin returned. He looked at her and, knowing she loved music, asked, "Do you like that song?"

"Yes, Min. It's lovely."

And, despite the challenges, this day was lovely too!

Last wish—horseback riding! Min invited Stephen and his wife to join.

The stable owner led us to the horses. She and her stablehand helped Min mount. Min rode between two guides who steadied him, making this wish-come-true a success and delight.

When Min expressed wanting to attend the Christmas parade in our former Kentucky mountain town, we planned an open house. The town offered their community room as a gift. Other dear folk catered much of the food.

Min learned we'd attend our old church that Sunday and asked, "Can I be baptized, and can Dad do it? The preacher-who-loves-Groundhog-Day is old. I'm tubby now. He might drop me. And can Stephen be with me since he helped me ask Jesus into my life?"

To our surprise and delight all three brothers and their families wanted to come. We made motel reservations and contacted our church family who, in turn, announced the weekend events to all.

Min talked about this non-stop. We also were excited to visit our adopted hometown! That Friday we gave Min medication for dizziness, headed east, then bedded down at the motel.

Rain canceled the parade. That didn't stop fire- and policemen from providing one just for Min and giving him mementos (which he treasures).

That night we turned in, exhausted yet blessed. Min chose to sleep on a floor mat because "it doesn't hurt to fall from the floor."

We awoke around midnight to Min's cries—like a distressed animal, banging his head on our bed—inconsolable, barely able to speak. We eventually grasped that his head hurt so badly he couldn't cope and nursed him till morning.

Min said he couldn't go through with the baptism but rallied some when we arrived at the church. The preacher told us the baptismal heater broke, and the water was "right cold." Min still wanted to try. Then he lay on a pew and slept.

Brian and I did special music, then I sat by Min with a grandbaby on my lap. That comforted me greatly. Brian guest-preached.

Min awoke near the end.

During the closing hymn, Brian, Stephen, and Min changed into robes and entered the baptismal. Min shivered as he testified that Jesus lived in his life.

Buried in baptism. Raised to walk in newness of life!

In the land of the living, Min checked off wishes—joy and sorrow intertwined.

Bucket List, one more—a visit to Colonel Sanders' grave! Min joked, "I should've brought a bucket of chicken. Is that funny?" He then wandered to another grave. He read the inscription aloud—"'I had a really good time.' I like that. Can that be on my tombstone or a Chinese take-out order with 'to be delivered?' Is that funny?"

Having a good time despite it all,
Min and his folks

| 32 |

Solving Difficult Mysteries

*"... the river will get you to your destination, but it
will take much longer ... God has a purpose for every bend ..."*
—*Glenn Frontin* (adoptive grandparent)[77]

During 2015 I improved with walking. I still had dizziness and balance issues. I used an electric cart at stores, and we bought a mobility scooter. My nieces and nephews liked getting rides.

My medi-port was removed, but no catheter for this surgery. I was happy that the alien port exited this earthling. Then more good news!

Our friends, Jeff and Marion, treated me to see the circus—another wish I hoped for. I loved everything about it, and they had food too. I was exhausted when we got home, but I went to bed with a smile.

In 2016 we learned my kids-oncologist was leaving. It would be hard finding another doctor who knew about my favorite cartoons and was very skilled about brains. I graduated to an adult doctor. His place was different. No toys or fish.

Our first appointment at the new place was super long, so they brought snacks and drinks. *I'll like this place.* Then a man came with a musical instrument and played for me.

I said, "Mom and Dad like music."

The man got instruments for them to play too.

This was a good day.

My new oncologist pursued his dreams. He joined an expedition to solve the mystery of Amelia Earhart's disappearance. He said helping brain cancer patients and searching for her were both complex puzzles. *I'm in good hands.*

But right now, my tumors were still asleep—great news for me—so the doctor had time for a good, long rest after his aviation mission.

This oncologist sent me for two hours of something called vestibular testing because dizziness and falling continued.

The testing lady put me in a big container like a short rocket. I counted down to blast-off while Mom and Dad sat outside watching my face on a screen and hearing me. The lady gave me instructions through a speaker into the "rocket."

I about went nuts in there and almost vomited. My eyeballs were like googly-eyes—shaking back and forth. I couldn't wait until it ended. I came out with bloodshot eyes, fighting to focus and balance myself. Then I glanced at my parents.

They looked sad. They told me later it was very hard knowing I suffered through that.

Next: balance tests. During that the lady told my parents, "I've seen the vestibular system become intoxicated from carboplatin." That's what happened to me, and it would take a long time to recover.

Mourning Dove—The Sequel,   Spring 2016

You're not the same bird that sang to our son nineteen years ago, but he thinks you are.

He hurries downstairs, forgetting he falls now. Plunk.

We call from the living room. "Are you okay?"

"Yeah." Min staggers in and gives us a little wave. (He always does this when coming into our view—several times each day,) "I have a friend! Remember when I was little and talked to the mourning dove in New York?"

"Yes."

"She's back! She made a nest at my window!"

We smile. "That's your friend?"

Min nods. "I'm so happy the bird chose my window. I love her there."

Our beautiful son—marred by life's hardships—listens to you from a nearby recliner where he rests on days that are too hard. Your song is still sad, but Min loves it and you. He just wanted a friend, and now he has one.

With a song from our hearts,

a rejoicing Dad and Mom

P.S.— Thank You, Creator, for sending this gift to Min. You knew just what he needed.

My parents noticed I struggled with short-term memory issues. Before my kids-oncologist left, she said the mass in my brain messed me up—like beginning dementia. My adult oncologist said therapies might help.

I started memory and balance therapies two times each week for six weeks. I didn't like memory therapy. They gave homework, but I liked balance therapy. The dude that worked with me was cool. We did challenges with a big electronic screen and skills at a table. This helped me, and there was a Chinese restaurant nearby.

One time the dude wanted me to make correct change without help. It took me many minutes, but I did it in my own unique way.

He had a baffled expression. "Wow! I don't know what your method was, but you got it correct!"

I conquered the problem and, in my opinion, earned a Chinese lunch. So I got one.

But another problem started. We thought it was a pimple because I got those since I was a teenager and didn't leave them alone. This "pimple" under the middle of my lower lip grew fast. *I'll take care of that thing!* I ripped it off. It bled gob loads into my hands. I quick went to my parents. I was a bloody mess, and they had trouble stopping the bleeding.

We went to my NF doctor. He sent us to a plastic surgeon. I don't know why he was called plastic, but he said the non-pimple was a fibroma. No surprise. That's what us NF1 people grow, but it needed to be removed. By the time I had surgery, it was as big as a pea.

I went for surgery and feared the catheter business, but I was spared that horror. The plastic doctor said the fibroma could grow back, but he thought he got it all. I had to be super careful while my under-lip healed. Eating was hard but necessary.

My blood pressure continued to be a problem. At this new location, I was matched with a nephrologist who wanted to solve this mystery.

The doctor introduced herself and said, "I'd like to help you, my friend."

I tipped my head like a wondering dog. "Friend? Aren't you my doctor?"

"Can I be both?"

"Yes. I would love that!" I was amazed and talked to her about My Little Pony. She didn't know much about that, but she sat and listened.

All of a sudden, I stuck my fingers in my ears.

Dr. Friend stood up quick, came over, and put her hand on my shoulder. "Are you okay?"

"He struggles with hearing high pitches we can't hear." Mom sounded like muffled-talk, but I knew she explained about my Asperger hearing.

"Let's get you into a quieter room!" Dr. Friend said.

I smiled big, picked up my stuff, and finished in a room that didn't squeal. This doctor was being my doctor and friend, just like she said.

I had tests then waited for results.

Dr. Friend—like Sherlock Holmes—solved my high blood pressure mystery, which had something to do with my brain. She changed my medicine and added a new one, and this magically improved me.

I wanted a job now that I wasn't sick all the time. *Maybe I can work at the zoo*, but it was too far. In my heart I still wanted to work with animals, but I wondered about other jobs.

For a while I wanted to be a police officer.

My parents said, "You're strong, but you'd struggle with quick judgment, speed in running, and fine motor use of your hands."

That made me mad, and I argued. When I got over that anger, I thought I could be a construction worker.

Mom asked, "How well do you do math?"

I put my hands on my hips. "That job requires math?"

"Yes, exact measuring and using power tools. What about balancing and not falling from high places?"

I was too grown up now to stomp my foot, but I felt like doing that. "My teachers told me I can be anything I want to be!"

"That's not actually true," Mom said.

I was shocked. "You mean it's a lie?"

"Well, yeah. The truth is you can be anything GOD wants you to be. He equips you with all you need to do His Will."

Hmm. I understand now.

After that I told my parents my ideas, but I didn't argue. And I learned to think what skills were needed for certain jobs. I realized some jobs I could never do, some I might learn to do, and some I can do.

Dear not-so-welcomed Grief,   *Dateline: Always*

We don't just go through you when dealing with death. We experience you with lost expectations. As Min grew, he fell further and further behind until we faced a mountain of accumulated losses.

Most kids eventually leave home. This son never will. He won't live without some supervision. He can't make all decisions himself but can have a say. He won't drive. We're his taxi always. He won't easily hold a job unless it's tailored for him.

Then this: Because of brain cancer, Min's slowly digressing—his memory waning. This burdens him. We grieve with him—for him—and sometimes become exhausted from it all, as does he. Then we regroup, state what's real now—not yesterday—and embrace this new normal, which isn't normal at all. But this is Min's life. And ours.

We're reminded: "Surely He hath borne our griefs and carried our sorrows ..." Isaiah 53:4a. [78] *God cares so much that He willingly continues bearing everything that grieves and causes us sorrow. What Love!*

So, Grief, one day you'll have us bawling at the ultimate mark of your existence—death. But you're no stranger, and—although we don't want you— we need you.

We just ask that you not crowd out the joys in each day. If this happens, we'll forget good lives here also. That we walk this journey for a reason. That it needed to be so. That God ordains our days and gives us the gift of releasing all hurts to God through you.

> *Sharing the journey,*
> *a continuing-on father and mother*

| 33 |

A New Home—A New Adventure

"... they that wait upon the Lord, shall renew their strength:
they shall lift up the wings, as the eagles ..." Isaiah 40:31a [79]

Summer 2018. We took a vacation to the Ozark Mountains in Missouri. On the way home I asked, "Could we move to Missouri? I like it a lot."

"Maybe." My parents didn't tell me this trip was to explore being missionaries there. They just said, "You can pray about it." I don't remember if I did because I have memory issues.

Weeks after we arrived home, Dad called a family meeting.

I came in the living room and gave a little wave.

Dad said, "Min, we've been praying about moving to Missouri for some months now. Our mission board okayed it. What are your thoughts?"

"I approve. The roads aren't curvy, people were nice, and they have interesting rocks."

Dad smiled. "Well, we're not going because of the rocks, but they are different from here. We think God is saying to go."

"Can I bring all my stuff? Will we be near a Chinese restaurant? Is Missouri closer to Chuck Norris?

Mom said, "How 'bout most of your stuff? Chinese restaurant? We'll see. And Chuck Norris? Yeah, a lot closer."

"Yes!" I pumped my fisted arm in a celebrating gesture.

We began getting our house ready to sell and started packing. Then my parents talked with my brothers—one family at a time. When they got to Stephen, they weren't sure what would happen because they moved here to help us.

Stephen and his wife breathed relief, and he said, "We weren't sure how to tell you, but we believe God's moving us too." So, it all worked out. They had their plan from God, and we had ours. These two families moved different directions early in 2019, but it was sad leaving the other families.

I didn't like things changing, but this time I was excited! We bought a house in a small town on a dead-end street where some police lived. I felt safe. There were kids to play with. The people were friendly and stopped to talk in stores, like when we lived in the Kentucky mountains. There was a Chinese restaurant too! I went there for my twenty-sixth birthday!

But I worried my desk would obstruct my bedroom door view because Jason, who called me Pappy, screamed "boo" five years ago.

Mom said, "Don't worry, it only happened once, and we're not the booing type."

But I was dead set on my desk's location because you never know about visitors.

We found all new doctors—a big accomplishment. We traveled for most appointments and MRIs. That's okay because sometimes we got Chinese take-out on the way home.

I stayed home when Mom and Dad visited churches to see which one we picked. Then I visited the final choices because of my sensory deprivation and brain cancer. I didn't function well in some churches.

Dear Little White Church,

When we started attending here, the pastor greeted us, then Min. "Hello, sir!"

Min, not a fan of "new," became flustered and fixed his eyes on me as he does when unsure.

I whispered, "Min, look at him. He's talking to you."

"But I don't know who he is."

"He's the pastor." I looked Pastor's way, attempting to fix this. "He's not sure who you are. People look alike to him."

Next, Pastor sat to our son's right. Min panicked! No one usually sat there.

I reached over and rubbed my fist down Min's spine to help him regain composure.

Just then Pastor said, "I have a joke for you."

Min's head whipped right.

Pastor told Min about an elephant with red painted toenails. Why? So it could hide in a cherry tree.

Our son smiled. "I have 5,000 jokes. I'll tell you one next Sunday."

At home, we explained the course joke-telling should take on the Lord's Day. "The pastor has many cares before the church service, so it isn't appropriate to tell him jokes then. Better to wait until afterward."

"That's the rule for jokes there?" Min questioned.

"Yes. More appropriate."

The next Sunday we reviewed the procedure.

Min repeated, "Jokes must wait until church ends."

We took our seats and readied for worship. Min opened his Bible and read.

Pastor came and stood near Min. "Hello, sir. I have a joke for you."

Min zeroed in on me and became anxious.

"Min, look at him. He wants to tell you a joke."

His anxiety increased. "But I don't know what to do. He's not being appropriate!"

There ya go, Little White Church! Your pastor's not always "conventional." Yet, he's won our son's heart.

Thus, we apologize for our son saying Pastor's not appropriate, but we're grateful for a shepherd who cares for and feeds his sheep—and our lamb.

Next, we thank you! One Sunday, as the song leader descended the platform after the closing hymn, our son—thumbing through the hymnal—asked her, "Do you have Horatio Spafford in here?"

"I'm not sure. Can you give me a clue who he is?"

Min lifted his head a bit. "He wrote 'It Is Well with My Soul.'"

"Oh yes! We love that hymn!" she said.

Our son smiled then explained about Mr. Spafford's tragic life.

And she listened.

The next Sunday, the song leader introduced the hymns, the last one being "It Is Well with My Soul." She glanced Min's way and smiled, but his head was buried in his Bible.

After the service, Min commented, "Did you hear? The lady picked my favorite song—the one I want at my funeral."

This dear lady, whom Min calls "the-woman-with-white-hair-from-church-who-shops-at-Walmart," touched our son that Lord's Day. He didn't react much. He usually doesn't, yet she blessed his day, and we thank her.

Don't close your doors yet, Church!

We were still new to you when at the close of a service Min plopped in the center aisle.

A few people approached, quite concerned.

"He'll be okay," I said. "He has brain cancer and falls sometimes."

Everyone was kind, caring, and didn't make Min feel uncomfortable. We carried on a little conversation until he was able to stand, then headed out.

*Without missing a beat, Min turned to the man at the door, who he now
knows is Pastor, and asked, "Do you have a joke for me?"*

Feelin' at home,

part of the family

In Missouri I needed new guardianship because my Kentucky
papers weren't good there and were expiring. I didn't mind still needing
guardians, and my parents wanted to be mine even though they were
getting old.

I wanted more than anything to vote. I knew right from wrong.
I can read about candidates and make wise choices.

The court hearing happened in February 2020. The judge granted
my wish to vote! I thanked him profusely!

Then Dad had surgery on his throat because strokes damaged his
vocal cords. He voice-trained every day to get better. I felt empathy for
his struggle, but this also showed me never to give up.

When COVID-19 lockdown happened, we landscaped and planted
a garden. I was good at that because I learned skills in my high school
landscaping class.

Mom wrote on fat popsicle sticks to label our seedlings.

I joked, "Why don't we label them all corn? That's what they
ended up with in *Secondhand Lions.* [80] Can we get a pet lion?"

Mom laughed.

We didn't get a lion, but we made a little backyard environment
called Toady Town that toads could call home because we had lots
of those.

March 9th, 2021. My birthday! A dream came true! My parents
gave me a two-wheel bike! I was joyful to ride again, like before my
brain biopsy and chemo. I rode and felt the wind in my face—free as a
bird, like one that visited us.

A golden eagle landed in our backyard. Then it spread ginormous wings and took flight with a snake in its claws. It flew into our nut tree then took off out of view. It was a wonderful sight full of amazement!

The eagle took off, and now so could I. It clutched the snake, but I clutched the handlebars. We both liked soaring and being free.

For ten years I was a guy without a camp. I always loved camp more than anything and missed this experience.

Then we learned about Camp Barnabas [81] for people like me. It was nearby. It cost a ton-load of money, but God helped me raise it all!

I was a camper again! There were many counselors from South Korea. I was over-the-moon with joy! I hadn't seen this many Koreans since leaving my homeland! I felt like I was home, and I jumped up and down! I asked them to sign my notebook, and they did!

When my parents picked me up, I talked-talked-talked about coming again. I loved camp so much!

Dear Superman—The Sequel,   *July 2021*

You can't believe what transferring guardianship to another state was like, even with laws to do this "with ease." Although it took ten months, Missouri recognized the need since Min was already "incapacitated." We and Min needed our own lawyers for court, but no jury or testing—just informal interviews.

On the court-appointed day, Min could take the stand if he wished. He declined. Our lawyer questioned us, as did the judge. Then he asked if there was anything further.

Min's lawyer stood. "Your Honor, my client wishes to be granted the right to vote."

"I will grant it." Then the judge summarized and pounded his gavel.

Done.

Min sat a little taller. *"He said I can vote! I'll be responsible and study and do a good job!"*

Min registered to vote in the 2020 election. Brian ran off a sample ballot, and Min reviewed a candidates' comparison list. After casting his vote, he proudly wore his *"I voted!"* sticker.

We're not done yet, Supe'. Fast forward: Summer 2021. Min attended a new special needs camp—Barnabas. Registration was held at several drive-through stops. At the camp-nurse stop, we answered questions, then Min did.

The nurse addressed Min. *"I'm sure you want to join the fun, but, before I let you go, do you have any questions for me?"*

"Aren't you going to ask me if Superman is real?"

There ya go, Supe'! Ten years passed, but the question remains: Are you real?

Beginning to wonder,

real Brian and real Sarah for real interesting Min

For a long while, my tumors were stable, then my MRI showed change. One of my three lesions—besides my tumors—started growing. It was at the back of my brain, so the good news was it could be removed if it grew more. Next MRI, though, showed no change. That's how my brain is for now.

But then I started having petit mal seizures. Maybe I had them before. We weren't sure. But now my head and eyes turned and I shook, so we went to the neurologist.

Another medicine that made me sleepy was added twice each day.

I began forgetting to take my meds. Sometimes I mixed up pills by mistake and put some in my pocket, thinking I would remember later.

I was at the dentist. She laid back my chair, and we heard "tcht—tcht, tcht—tcht." Mom's face turned red, and the dentist picked up my meds. I apologized, hoping that stopped Mom's lecture on the way home, but I got one anyway. Then I realized I put myself in danger.

My parents bought a pill box with an alarm and flashing lights to help me. This discouraged me at first because it felt like going backwards. But later I like that it helped me and that someone invented this cool item.

| 34 |

Missing Pieces

"I am a secret that can never be revealed.
A secret that she buried ..." —*Lori Wagner Knisely* (adoptee)[82]

After my brain cancer diagnosis, I desperately wanted to find my birth parents. How much time did I have left? I'm like a bomb that would explode—"tic...tic...tic"—like slow motion with every frame of movie film building suspense and anxiety! I wanted to disarm it, but I couldn't.

We contacted AIAA Post Adoption Services to help. We moved then, Mom still had some pneumonia, and I was horribly sick from chemo for more than two years. Maybe that's why, but we never got search papers to sign. Then AIAA closed down. What would we do?

We could try searching when we settled in Missouri.

My parents worked on their family trees. I googled information, and Mom filled in huge charts. It was fun, and I earned pay.

I became curious about these people and their stories. "Are there any adopted people?"

"Yes. Here," Mom pointed then traced her finger to another name, "and here."

"Neat!" I smiled then lowered my head. "Are there any people like me?"

"Disabled?"

I shook my head.

"Oh, born to unwed parents?"

I nodded.

Mom pointed to another name. "One of my many-times great-grandmothers was what they called a 'bastard child.'"

My mouth went agape. "I can't believe you said that!"

"Back then that's the word that meant illegitimate. A child born to an unmarried woman was recorded that way."

This helped me with feelings about how I became me. I wasn't alone.

Then I thought more about my birth parents. *Who do I look like? Did my birth parents marry other people and I have half-siblings? Are they alive?* I desperately needed to know. "Tic...tic...tic..."

The only thing I knew about my birth parents' looks was how tall they were. Mom measured the height of my birth mother, drew a pencil line, and wrote "Kim" on my bedroom door frame. She added my birth father's height and labeled it "Cho." Then my height with "Min." I was taller than my mother even though I'm short because of NF1, but not as tall as my birth father. I liked this reminder.

I did a DNA test, which came back full Asian heritage with one distant cousin match. Maybe in time other blood family would do DNA and be added.

But the odds were against me finding my birth parents. Less than 3% of Korean adoptees (in my generation) find theirs.[83] Would I find mine?

Dearest Birth Mother,   *September 2021*

Not long ago I learned of a birth mother and her story, surrendering her baby to adoption. My heart broke for her, even though she reunited with her child and is well beyond that now.

When I asked if we could meet, she pleasantly agreed. I admitted I hadn't realized the deep grief a birth mother felt—wondering where her baby was, knowing she might never see her child again. I'd been clueless about the heartache, guilt, and longing.

She shared book titles, and I read more birth mothers' stories—all so similar. When the reading became too difficult to bear, I closed the book. It felt wrong. Could these women put aside their anguish?

Then I read I WISH FOR YOU A BEAUTIFUL LIFE ... Korean birth mothers' letters to their babies [84] and imagined these matched your heart cry.

I'm writing, first, to say I'm sorry. I saw surrendering a child as matter-of-fact (in light of overwhelming numbers of adopted post-war Korean babies). In my thinking you had little choice, picked the best for your baby, and moved on with life.

Secondly, I admire your courage. I don't imagine it felt like that to you, but from our point of view, you're a heroine. You could have legally ended your pregnancy early on. Maybe you considered ending your life. Many birth mothers express these feelings. Why would you differ because you live half-a-world away?

Thirdly, thank you for giving your baby life. Did you see your son at birth? Spend days with him while awaiting to sign for international adoption? Did you choose his name because it bore special significance?

I cannot imagine what your life has been—wondering about your child, wishing for some word. Many birth mothers share not a day passes without thoughts of their babies. I thought you might only think of Min Soo on his birthday. How naïve I was!

After researching South Korean laws, we realized we must search for you—knowing you're unable to. Now Min Soo is doing this, hoping to find you. We pray he does.

When you are found, you'll learn your son has lived through great difficulties, but God has showered him with much good. You can be proud of your son. He is kind, compassionate, and—although struggles with disability— knows right from wrong and values others. His heart is oh so tender.

Dearest Birth Mother, may all the years' hardnesses be erased when you're found and told, "Your son wants to meet you." Until then, we pray this becomes reality.

Honoring you in my heart,
Sarah (adoptive mother)

Who would help me search? We needed to pray, so I did.

"Lord, could you please help me find my birth parents? In Jesus' Name, Amen."

United States—Summer 2021

Mom and Dad find an online Korean adoption site. They ask if any adoptees searched for birth parents and who helped. Most people say SWS. We contact them. Dad sets up e-mail for me because they want to communicate through me.

South Korea: August 17th, 2021

SWS assigns me a case worker. That person writes to make sure I'm me.

United States—August 18th, 2021. 10:21 a.m.

I write e-mail: "This is Kim Min Soo and my adoption number is 93-89 SHK. My most desire is to find my birth parents. My father who is named Cho, ___ ___ and my mother Kim, ___ ___. I have brain cancer and disability. I want to find them before it's too late. Can you please help me? Sincerely Kim, Min Soo—Birthday March-9-1993" [ss]

September 10th, 2021

We collect required documents. Dad sends them to Post Adoption Services. Mom helps me fill in search paperwork because I don't understand it.

October 20th, 2021

We send a letter from my oncologist so SWS understands I'm seriously ill.

South Korea—November 8th, 2021

SWS needs more documents. It will take time to search because they give everything to a Korean government agency for rights of children.

United States—same week

We send more documents. I must write a letter agreeing to accept search results no matter what they are. It can be bad, but I hope it's good.

Seoul, South Korea—November 30th, 2021. 8:04 p.m.

E-mail from South Korea: My birth mother is located, not in Pusan—place of my birth, but in another region. My birth father isn't located, and no records are found.

They will send a registered letter to my supposed-to-be birth mother to make sure she is the right person because 20% of South Korea have family name Kim.[85] The law allows them to send three letters only.

SWS sends child study notes about my birth parents and infant-me. My birth mother went with friends to Pusan and worked at a shoe factory. A friend introduced my birth parents, and they lived together about two years. Their employer let them live in a room.

My birth parents wanted to get married, but my birth father's parents were "strongly opposed." In Korean culture, parents make the rules. Many adult children won't go against them. I don't know if that was before or after my birth father learned my birth mother was pregnant. My birth father "cut off contact with her giving her some money for child delivery ..." and left his job. [tt]

I was utterly surprised my birth father cared enough to give my birth mother money to deliver me. He cared! Before I hated him because I thought he walked away. Now I know he loved my birth mother; but family heritage, culture, and tradition made an impossible decision for him. This would shatter his heart—stuck between two different loves.

My birth mother reported she was honest and good-natured. She said my birth father was tidy, neat-looking, and outgoing. Some of me is like their personalities. My birth mother also shared about their looks. I am like both. My face is shaped like my birth mother, and my eyes and nose are like my birth father.

When my birth mother sent me up for adoption and I went to Seoul, the court appointed me a guardian as "Acceptance of Abandoned Child."

I'm listed in the South Korean Family Register as "family head"— "no record" of "relationship with the former family head," "no record" of father, also "no record" of mother. This is horrible—nightmare-inducing!

In my homeland, if I don't have blood-ties to "former family head," I cannot be real in the Family Register, my link to citizen rights in the land of my birth. My roots were cut—just like other adoptees sent internationally—because to be adopted inside my homeland, they need blood-line ties not to be ostracized.[86]

Same Day—United States

The best news I ever heard! The woman who was located is my mother! I want to make her a necklace for Christmas and send a picture of me. I hope she sends a picture. If I can't meet in person, I want to know what she looks like. I hope this happens by Christmas. That would be the best present ever!

Christmas 2021

No news, but I still hope. Mom and Dad give me historical Korean decorations to add to my memorabilia—copies from the Shilla Dynasty when Kims ruled. Kim means "gold." I like that and also that my ancestors were rulers.

Seoul, South Korea—January 10th, 2022

The case worker sends me e-mail. My mother called SWS. She is married and never told any family about me, so she cannot get in touch with me but will call the agency later. The agency will contact me immediately when they hear from her again.

Same Night—United States. 9:59 p.m.

I emoted shaky-happiness that my mother responded to the SWS letter but was also grief-stricken with sadness because she won't be in touch with me now. I sat in my desk chair, slid down with my head thrown back. Tears came but didn't fall. I tried to process this. My breathing shook like hyperventilating, and I stared at the ceiling. My lamenting sunk me into deep waters where sorrow weighed me down. I felt no one could rescue me.

I waited almost twenty-nine years for this moment. I always felt my heart connected to my mother, and I thought she would be eager to see me because she left clues when she put me up for adoption—full name, birthplace, age, place of family origin.

But my mother was married now. That changed everything. I was a secret this whole time—all my years plus my time inside her. She never told anyone except my father. When I was born, I was nothing. *Am I still nothing?* My mother's secret was as dark as deep ocean waters, and I was buried—like bones or a treasure.

Most Korean unwed mothers keep the birth secret out of fear of never having life back in society. If their secret gets out, they're ostracized and cannot hope for marriage. My mother is a victim of Korean traditional culture (so am I). That's why she kept me a secret.

Maybe my mother buried the secret—me—so she could find me later—like a treasure hunt with a map. She didn't know she would marry, but I think girls wish that and boys do too. That's why I had to be a secret. Not because she didn't love me, but because she gave me life, put me in good hands, and hoped a good life for me. Maybe that helped her keep living. But for her to keep living, I must stay buried.

My parents came in my room and sat on my bed. We talked and tried to figure good and bad from this news. They thought, because my mother called the agency, she needed time to deal with emotions and what to do about her husband. Would culture win or my mother's heart?

If a person doesn't fit into strict Korean social laws, they're outcasts. If an unwedded woman had a baby then marries and has other children and tells her secret, the new family most often breaks apart. Then more people have pain to bear.[87]

United States—March 9th, 2022

My birthday. I'm twenty-nine. Maybe my mother will respond today. She must be thinking about me.

South Korea—

United States—

I wait, check e-mail every day, and hope. "Tic…tic…tic…"

Keeper of our Tears,   *September 2022*

We need You, Lord! For You heal the brokenhearted and crushed in spirit.

Min didn't get what he wanted—first for Christmas, then his birthday. He seemed fine, until one night when he burst into our room, flooded with tears and with great urgency in his voice. You were there to dry his tears. "I need to know if my mother has Jesus in her life!"

"We don't know that, but we can pray she will if she hasn't already. Also, that God gives you peace."

"I'll be okay not meeting her on earth if I know that. I can wait. But I still want her picture. That would be enough."

I tried to understand the depth of our son's turmoil and equate it to— what? When this sunk in, it pierced me! Does Min need to do what his birth mother did when she let him go? If so, how do we handle such an agonizing conversation? I sought Your help. You were there to dry my tears. I mulled this in my mind a half year.

The day arrived, though, when out of the blue—while parked, awaiting a food order—Min brought up the subject. "If I visit Korea, I could meet my mother in secret."

"I'm not sure, under the circumstances, she'd take that risk." How could I speak these next words without hurting him? But I had to. "Min, might you need to do what your birth mother did for you? She gave you to adoption so you'd have a better life—surely the hardest decision of her life. Is it possible it's your turn?"

He looked at me in a half-understanding sort of way. "So she can keep her now-family?"

I nodded as tears welled.

He stared out the car window. Drawn-out moments passed.

"She risks losing everything if she acknowledges you," I said.

"But then she'd have me."

"Would she though? You're here, and she doesn't know you."

Minutes passed. You held our son.

"If I need to give my mother up to save her life with her now-family, I'll sacrifice her."

Min's words gripped me. "That may be the case."

Our son willingly returned a gift he hadn't received—the one he'd wanted more than anything.

He looked my way again and with a tiny shrug and voice of innocence said, "Well, I think this is what they call a lose/lose situation."

My lips trembled. "I suppose it is."

Keeper of Min's tears, his sorrows matter to You. One day You will wipe them all away. But for now, You weep with him and accept his offering—the mother he longs to know and his wet, salty tears. [uu]

Weeping also,

ones who grieve with You

FYI:

[ss] Min's typed e-mail

[tt] From Min's Korean child study received in 2021

[uu] From Psalm 34:18, Psalm 56:8, Rev. 21:4

| 35 |

One Step Closer to Home

"When I think of heaven, I think of a time
when I will be welcomed home."
—*Joni Eareckson Tada* (person with disability)[88]

Since I visited the Creation Museum petting zoo, I dreamed of working with animals. In 2021 a petting zoo opened. We went, and I loved it.

The zoo was for all kids, but the owner had experience with special needs kids and made sure they can have fun without fear. It calmed me.

Then Mom saw an ad online. The owner was hiring someone to socialize with the animals and help with their care. *My dream job!* We called right away, and I went for an interview. I did a month trial then became a fully accepted zoohand. I was flabbergasted! This filled my heart with joy!

I love being around the animals, and I'm good socializing with them. There was a scared peacock. My boss taught me how to calm it. I approached it, grasped its legs, wrapped my hand over it, and held it close so it felt secure. It looked franticly about and wanted to escape. I petted it and whispered, "It's okay. It's okay." Then it calmed.

My employer said she trusts me and I take good care of the animals. This means a lot to me.

I'm nervous before my oncology appointments when we get MRI results, and I randomly talk.

We drove to my appointment on a sunny day with lots of interesting clouds. I like cloud formations and weather phenomena. I looked up and pointed. "That one looks like a swan."

Mom quick glanced. "Yeah, or a galloping horse. I guess swans and horses look alike."

"They do when they're clouds." I thought a little. "Do you have trypophobia?"

"Haven't got a clue. What's it mean?"

"People who are afraid of holes," I explained.

Mom laughed. "I eat Swiss cheese, so I guess not."

"Why didn't you name me Amadeus?"

Mom's eyes looked surprised. "Never crossed our minds."

"Did you think of naming me Mephibosheth because of the story of David and him?"

"Nope. Too hard to spell."

"Yeah," I said. "I'm twenty-nine now, and I asked God to help me live to be thirty. Now it's pretty close. Can I ask Him for an extension?"

"Sure," Mom said.

"I'm already older than Robert Germain Thomas when he died in Korea."

"How do you know about him?" Mom asked.

"*Torchlighters* DVDs [89] about martyrs. He was a missionary."

"I'd like to see that. How 'bout we watch it with Dad?"

I gave Mom a thumbs up.

The next week we watched it. Robert Germain Thomas went to Korea to give out Bibles secretly because Korea was hostile to outsiders. He escaped danger months later. But he had a heart burden and returned with more Bibles on a ship. It all went bad.

Before Robert was killed, he threw Bibles overboard so they wouldn't burn and made it to shore calling out, "Yesu, Yesu,"—"Jesus, Jesus" in Korean.

Another person who took part in this killing business destroyed a Bible and glued the pages to a wall in his house to brag about his victory. Years later people read them and asked Jesus into their lives. That's how Korea eventually became a Christian nation.

I'm thankful for Robert Germain Thomas because about one hundred years later his influence remained. A Korean girl asked Jesus into her life. She became a woman with great faith who knew prayer was important—my omma who prayed for me.

Robert didn't quit his purpose. His story inspires me to keep living. He showed that one person can change a nation.

I wonder, when I die, if my life's work will have any effect.

"When my father and mother forsake me, then the Lord will take me up." Psalm 27:10 [90]

I felt like I was sunk in the deep darkness of ocean waters (where Mariana snailfish dwell) when my mother said she cannot contact me. But Jesus rescued me because to Him I'm a treasure, and He is familiar with rescuing. It's not His first time.

When my birth parents left me, God sent me to a foster mother. Not just anyone. He Hand-picked Mrs. Choi. She fought to keep me from being sent to the orphanage for "hard cases." She devotedly prayed for me. I was in God's Hands the whole time because He placed me in a Christian family, like Mrs. Choi prayed.

Dear Dad and Mom,
    I'm happy you took me in as your son. I love you.
        Your beloved son,
          Min

After I had an adoptive Christian family, I learned more about what Jesus did for me. A simple way I understood was "A" for accept Jesus is God and also my salvation. "B" for believe in my heart and ask Him into my life. "C" for confess sins. That meant I needed to say, "I'm sorry I did those sins, and I know You're my Lord."

I did that, and Jesus forgave me and came into my life. He adopted me—I was rescued. This gave me hope and purpose. Heaven's gates were opened for me. One day I'll be welcomed Home and free from all I went through. Heaven is my satisfaction.

When we traveled to the neurologist because of my seizures, we had another good talk.

"In Heaven, I want to be child-like, like I am now."

Mom smiled.

"I don't want to go to Heaven until you and Dad do—or die in my sleep. I hope that's how it happens."

"We don't decide that. God already knows when and how we'll go."

"But I want to stay together."

"Time in Heaven will seem different. The Bible says a thousand years there is like a day. If you go first, you'll walk around meeting everyone and talking up a storm. Then you'll feel someone tap your shoulder, but it won't scare you because you won't have Asperger's any-more. When you turn around, you'll see one of us and say, 'Oh, you're here already?'"

"But I wish I wasn't going to die. Sometimes I'm afraid."

"Actually, you're not going to," Mom said. "You'll just get a new address and leave your sick, disabled body behind because you don't need it. Before you finish one fast blink, you'll be there in your new body."

"I'm going to see President Lincoln, President Reagan, people from the biblical era, C.S. Lewis, Fanny J. Crosby (she can see), all my grandparents, the martyrs, Uncle Rick, Gladys Aylward, Corrie ten Boom, the little boy from fourth grade who doesn't have cancer now. Jess's great-grandmother, George Mueller ..."

"There are so many," Mom said. "You'll have such wonderful conversations, and you'll not only be friends but family too."

"Can I pray and ask God what Heaven is like?"

"He's already told you." Mom said.

I put my thumb and pointer finger across my chin. "How?"

"In the Bible. You can read all about Heaven."

"Like streets of such pure gold you can see through them? And twelve gates—each one made from one pearl? And the glass-looking sea by the throne?"

"Do you remember when Pastor preached about the rainbow around God sitting on the throne?" [vv]

"Yeah, like the brockenspectre." [91]

Mom looked surprised. "Sounds like you already have a pretty good idea what Heaven's like."

I hugely smiled. "And I won't have a big head."

"Right. No NF1 and no seizures either."

"In Heaven with my sensory issues gone, my vision will see God. My hearing will love the angels singing without wearing sound-blocking headphones. My smell will know when the feast food is ready, and my taste will make me want seconds because there's enough for everyone—Look what Jesus did with the fish and bread! My touch won't mind Jesus hugging me and me hugging Him back.

When I feel sick and dizzy and I'm having a hard day, I want to go to Heaven.

Then I start to feel better and remember I have a purpose, a mission to complete. That's why I think God still has me here. When my purpose is completed, then I'll go to Heaven, and that will be my final Home."

"Kkeut"
(Korean for "The End")

FYI:
[vv] Referencing Revelation 4:2-3

CONCLUSION

Dear Reader,

Why God picked us from all the people in the world to adopt Min is a wonder. All we can say is a precious woman (then 6,688 miles away) prayed for a home for Min Soo, and we offered him a seat at our table. God orchestrated the rest.

As we researched old notes, letters, and records, at times Min said, "I was so much trouble. Didn't you think you should send me back?"

"No. Never."

"It would be easier without me."

"But not right. We often thought 'this is very hard' but never thought of sending you back."

We didn't spend more than two hours a day writing. More was physically burdensome for Min. There were times his words flowed and others when he only formed a handful of sentences. Yet he's not wavered in his commitment to tell his story. He's proved a faithful soldier to the task, and we're proud of him.

It's been an exhausting, joyful, troubling, meaning-filled, difficult, wonderful path. We pray Min's story helps you discover peace where God has placed you. As Min says, "Sometimes you just have to be at a place—because God wants you there. It's your purpose."

For the glory of God,
Min's family

A DREAM COME TRUE

March 9th, 2023—GOD answered my prayer!
Happy 30th birthday to me!

For More information about Min Hampshire:

Facebook—Kim Min Soo, Author
Amazon—Author Central
E-mail: ahomeforminsoo@gmail.com
Youtube.com/ahomeforminsoo

ACKNOWLEDGEMENTS

"Gamsahamnida"

(Korean for "Thank You")

GOD, You gave me life and helped me tell my story. Thank You!

Thomas Hampshire, you helped me understand what I was like as a tot in my brand-new country.

Sharon Fieker Cummins, you shared your experience so I could understand my birth mother's point of view.

Nancy Fox, Bruce Behr, & Wendy Lucas, you made my adoption possible.

Mrs. Colelli, Mrs. Burns, Mrs. Jones, & Mrs. Fleming, thank you for being my aides even though I was a difficult child.

Mr. "Family," my special ed teacher and very good friend, thank you.

Friends & family, you prayed and cheered me on!

Seon Joo So, you helped us much with translating.

Nita Hickman, your support helped me.

Diana Lee Flegal, thank you for believing in me and my story before I started writing and then becoming my agent. My prayer has been answered through you.

Eddie Jones, you did great coaching to get my book published.

Pamela Hedberg, Eileen Mackintosh, Sharon Fieker Cummins, Deborah Sisk, Richard Kee, & Gene Arthur Sabatino, you gave much preview-reading time.

Trisha White Priebe, you gave your time and soul to write my foreword.

Phyllis Smith and Constance McKnight Cloud, you did a great job proofreading.

Hannah Linder, thank you for the tremendous cover design!

Delaney Hampshire, you are a gift God sent for me.

NOTES

ONE

[1] Steve Morrison, "The Heart of an Orphan," *MPAK—Mission to Promote Adoption of Kids* (founded 1999), 10/28/2020, https://www.facebook.com/mpakusa/posts/10158703635599723. Used with permission.

[2] Brian Boyd, *When You Were Born in Korea* (1368 Michelle Drive, St. Paul MN 55123: Yeong & Yeong Book Company, 1993), p. 5.

TWO

[3] *The Flintstones*, "Little Bamm-Bamm," 10/3/1063 on ABC, Hanna Barbera Productions—Screen Gems.

[4] *Looney Tunes*, "Merrie Melodies Series," ABC, Warner Brothers, 1954 (3400 Warner Blvd., Burbank CA 91505).

[5] Jung Hee Choi, "During I Raise Lovely Boy, Min Soo," *Social Welfare Society (SWS)*, Summer 1996 issue, pp. 4-5 (English translation by Jun Seo Hong & Jeon Joo So) (7 18-35 Yeoksam-dong, Gangnam-gu, Seoul, 135-080, Republic of Korea).

[6] Staff writer, "A Home for Min Soo," *Neurofibromatosis Ink*, Vol. 6 No. 1, Spring 1995, p.1 (8855 Annapolis Road—Suite # 110, Lanham MD 20706-2924: Neurofibromatosis, Inc.).

THREE

[7] Andrew C. Nahm Ph.D., B.J. Jones Ph.D., Gi-eun Lee, *I Love Korea* (400 Market Street, Suite #400: Philadelphia PA 19106, Jessica Kingsley Publishers, 2002), p. 64.

[8] Livingston Taylor, *Can I Be Good?* Ill. Ted Rand (San Diego, CA: Voyager Books—Harcourt Brace & Company, 1993).

FOUR

[9] Pat Boone, "Hoomania" Theme Song, *Hoomania*, ©1985, Adelphi Productions, https://m.youtube.com/watch?v=3jAdlvO_m3o&t=45s, 00:57-00:59.

FIVE

[10] E.B. White, *Stuart Little*, ill. by Garth Williams (557 Broadway, New York, NY 10019: Scholastic Inc., 1973), p. 9.

SIX

[11] Psalm 118:6 (KJV).

[12] *Gaither's Pond*, Benjy Gaither and Amy Hayes, (Gaither Studios & Live Bait Productions, © 1997-2003).

[13] Deuteronomy 3:22 (KJV).

SEVEN

[14] Linda Walvoord Girard, *Adoption is for Always*, ill. Judith Friedman (6340 Oakton Street, Morton Grove, IL 60053: Albert Whitman & Company, 1986), unnumbered pages.

[15] John McCutcheon, *Happy Adoption Day!* ill. Julie Paschkis (New York, NY: Little Brown and Company, 1996), unnumbered pages.

EIGHT

[16] Stephanie Fast, *She Is Mine* (P.O. Box 6081, Aloha, OR 97007: D.N.S. Publishing—Destiny Ministries, 2014), p. 178.

[17] "Veggie Tales," Phil Vischer and Mike Nawrocki (Big Idea Entertainments, ©1993).

[18] Claire Cloninger & Gary Rhodes, "He's Alive!: Celebration of the Living Lord," © 1/1/1995, Word Music, 25 Music Square W., Nashville TN 37203, cantata.

NINE

[19] Lucy Maud Montgomery, *Anne of Green Gables* (387 Park Avenue South, New York, NY 10016: Sterling Publishing Company, Inc., 2004), p. 235.

[20] BCM International, Inc. (Bible Centered Ministries)—formerly Bible Club Movement, founded 1936 by Miss Bessie Traber (201 Granite Run Drive—Suite 260, Lancaster PA 17601).

[21] *Barney and Friends*, HIT Entertainment, original air date 4/6/1992, PBS (675 Avenue of the Americas, New York, NY).

TEN

[22] C.S. Lewis, *Letters to Children* (866 Third Avenue, New York, NY 10022: Macmillan Publishing Company, 1985), p. 53.

[23] *Scooby-Doo, Where Are You!* Joe Ruby & Ken Spears—creators, 9/13/1969 original air date, CBS (Burbank CA: Warner Bros. Entertainment, Inc.).

[24] *Toy Story*, dir. John Lasseter (Guggenheim, Pixar Animation Studios / released by Walt Disney Pictures, 1995).

[25] *The Flintstones*, season 1—episode 1, "The Flintstone Flyer," 9/30/1960 original air date, ABC (3400 Cahuenga Blvd., Los Angeles, CA: Hanna Barbera, 1960).

ELEVEN

[26] Rudyard Kipling, *The Jungle Book*, ill. J. Lockwood Kipling, C.I.E. & W. H. Drake (20 New Wharf Road, London N19RR, UK: Macmillan Children's Books—an imprint of Pan Macmillan, 2016), p. 24.

[27] "George W. Bush's bullhorn speech," *American Rhetoric: Rhetoric of 9/11*, 9/14/2001 air date, https://www.americanrhetoric.com/speeches/gwbush911groundzerobullhorn.htm.

TWELVE

[28] Robert O'Rourke, *What God Did for Zeke the Fuzzy Caterpillar*, ill. John Ham (Cincinnati, OH: Standard Publishing Company, 1980).

[29] *The Lord of the Rings: The Fellowship of the Ring*, dir. Peter Jackson (New Line Cinema/WingNut Films, 2001), prod. Barrie M. Osborne, Peter Jackson, Fran Walsh, Tim Sanders, voice of Smeagol—Andy Serkis.

THIRTEEN

[30] Michael Bond, *A Bear Called Paddington*, ill. by Peggy Fortnum (195 Broadway, New York, NY 10007: Harper Collins Publishers, 1958), p. 8-9.

FOURTEEN

[31] Kathy Hoopmann, *All Cats Have Asperger Syndrome* (400 Market Street, Suite #400, Philadelphia, PA 19106: Jessica Kingsley Publishers, 2006), p. 7-8.

[32] Carol Stock Kranowitz M.A., *The Out-Of-Sync Child* (375 Hudson Street, New York, NY 10014: Berkley Publishing Group, 1998).

FIFTEEN

[33] Elizabeth Elaine Watson, *God Didn't Put Elephants Up in Trees*, ill. Dean Shelton (Nashville, TN: Broadman Press, 1981), p. 22.

SIXTEEN

[34] Isaac Watts, "False Greatness", *The Poetical Works of Isaac Watts and Henry Kirke White—With a Memoir of Each* (Boston: Houghton, Mifflin, and Company, the Riverside Press, Cambridge, digitized by Internet Archive, pub. date 1753, book date 1864, digitized 2017), p.159, https://achive.org/details/poeticalworksofi00watt_0ark:/13960/t6742qj131112.

SEVENTEEN

[35] Corrie ten Boom, *Common Sense Not Needed—Some Thoughts about an Unappreciated Work among Neglected People* (Fort Washington, PA 19034: Christian Literature Crusade, 1972), p. 22.

[36] *Crescendo*, written & dir. Alonso Alvarez Barreda—also written by Leo Severino, (Movie to Movement Production in assoc. with Wama Films & Noble Pictures—A Metanoia Films Production, released 11/28/2015).

[37] Korean Orphan Choir—World Vision, Inc., founded 1950 by Bob Pierce, P.O. Box 9716, Federal Way WA 98063.

[38] *Hollywood Talent Scout Show*, host Art Linkletter, Korean Orphan Choir, 12-27-1965, CBS, https://www/youtube.com/watch?v=DWwME6VA75A.

[39] Ludwig Van Beethoven, "Moonlight Sonata" (1801—*Piano Sonata No. 14 in C-sharp minor*), "Für Elise" (1810—*Bagatelle No. 25in A-minor for solo piano*), "Ode to Joy" (1824—*Symphony No. 9 in D-minor, Opus 125*).

EIGHTEEN

[40] Cleo A. Lampos, *A Mother's Song* (USA: Oak Tara Publishers, 2013), p. 123-124. Used with permission.

[41] Paul McCusker & Phil Lollar, *Adventures in Odyssey*, first aired 11/21/1987, Focus on the Family—James Dobson, founder—1977, Southern CA, now located at 8605 Explorer Drive, Colorado Springs, CO 80920.

[42] *American Hero Classics*, "The Wright Brothers," Brian Nissen, ©1996, HBO, Nest Family Entertainment, Rich Animation Studios, Animated Hero Classic, 4920 McDermott Rd.—Suite #200, Plano, TX 75024.

[43] *Adventures in Odyssey*, "Karen," audio CD album #3—track #8, "Heroes," © 11/26/1988 original air date.

[44] *Adventures in Odyssey*, "It Is Well," audio CD album #16—track #9, "Flights of Imagination," © 2/27/1993 original air date.

NINETEEN

[45] Naoki Higashida, *The Reason I Jump*, ©2007, (New York, NY: Pub. in English by Random House, NY, 2007), p. 4.

[46] *Adventures in Odyssey*, "East Winds, Raining," audio CD album #12—track #9, "At Home and Abroad," © December 7th, 1991 original air date.

[47] A.A. Milne, *Winnie the Pooh*, ill. E.H. Shepard (London, UK: Methuen & Co., 1926).

TWENTY

[48] Ted Geisel (Dr. Seuss Enterprises, L.P.), *Oh, the Places You'll Go!* (New York, NY: Random House Children's Books—a division of Random House, Inc., 1990), unnumbered pages.

[49] Stephen Hillenburg—creator, *SpongeBob SquarePants*, ©1999, owned by Nickelodeon.

TWENTY-ONE

[50] Jeremiah 29:11 (Geneva 1599).

TWENTY-TWO

[51] Psalm 121:2-3 (Geneva 1599).

[52] Michael Pellowski, *The Biggest Joke Book Ever (No Kidding)*, (12 Port Farm Road, Kennebunkport, ME 04046: Appleseed Press Book Publishers, LLC—imprint of Cider Mill Press Book Publishers, 2011).

TWENTY-THREE

[53] Doris Van Stone, *The Girl Nobody Loved*, with Erwin W. Lutzer (Chicago, IL: Moody Press—Moody Bible Institute, 1979), p. 146.

[54] *The Greatest Adventure: Stories of the Bible*, "Moses"—Episode #3, William Hanna & Joseph Barbera, Warner Video, Warner Bros., 4000 Warner Blvd., Burbank CA 91522, original air date December 1st, 1985 (added to YouTube 11/20/2007).

[55] Kentucky Raceway Ministries, Inc. (KRM), J.T. Marsh executive director, 10893 US-421, Milton, KY 40045.

[56] John 11:1-45 (KJV).

TWENTY-FOUR

[57] Sergio Cariello—author/ill., *The Action Bible* (4050 Lee Vance View, Colorado Springs, CO 80918: David C. Cook, 2009).

TWENTY-FIVE

[58] Psalm 23:6 (KJV).

TWENTY-SEVEN

[59] Charles D. Tillman, "When I Get to the End of the Way," *Evening Light Songs* (Guthrie, Oklahoma: Faith Publishing House, 1949). Public domain.

TWENTY-EIGHT

[60] Andrew C. Nahm Ph.D., B.J. Jones Ph.D., & Gi-eun Lee, *I Love Korea*, p. 14.

[61] Philadelphia Museum of Art, https://www.philamuseum.org/exhibitions/2014/795.html?page=3.

[62] John Francis Wade (attributed), "O Come All Ye Faithful" ("Adeste Fideles"), written 1744, (Lancashire, UK: Stonyhurst College, 1751), public domain.

TWENTY-NINE

[63] Trisha White Priebe, "God Wastes Nothing," *Lifesong for Orphans* (blog), 11-24-2021, https://lifesong.org/2021/11/right-where-you-belong/.

[64] Tom Wilson, *Ziggy* (1130 Walnut Street, Kansas City MO 64106: Andrews McMeel Publishers, launched 1968/syndicated 6/1/1971).

THIRTY

[65] Horatio G. Spafford (words) & Philip P. Bliss (music), "It Is Well With My Soul" (written in 1873, pub. 1876) Stamps-Baxter Music, completed 1876, (101 Winners Circle, Brentwood, TN: Brentwood-Benson Music Publishing, Stamps-Baxter Music, 1989), p. 299, public domain.

[66] Answers in Genesis, founder Ken Ham—1994, 2800 Bullittsburg Road, Petersburg, KY 41080.

[67] Buddy Davis, affiliated with Answers in Genesis, "Creation Adventures Team," ©2003.

[68] *Tom and Jerry*, Episode #57, original air date 4/7/1951, CBS, creators William Hanna & Joseph Barbera, MGM, https://m.youtube.com/watch?v=4_P-EDvsPOE.

THIRTY-ONE

[69] Joshua 1:9 (Geneva 1599).

[70] *SpongeBob SquarePants*, episode #15b, "The Suds," aired 1/17/2000, prod. Stephen Hillenburg, Albie Hecht, Julie Pistor, owned by Nickelodeon.

[71] "Jenkins parade honors young man battling cancer," WKYT, channel 27, CBS affiliate and The CW, aired 12/6/2014, ©2002-2022, A Gray Media Group, Inc. Station, Gray Television, Inc., 2851 Winchester Rd., Lexington, KY 40509.

[72] KEN HUB, https://www.kenhub.com/en/library/anatomy/the-brainstem.

[73] Britannica.com, https://www.britannica.com/science/midbrain.

[74] "Ill man, 21, gets wish for parade," *The Mountain Eagle*, 12/10/2014, ©1956, established 1907, 41 N. Webb Street, Whitesburg, KY 41858. https://www.the-mountaineagle.com/articles/ill-man-21-gets-wish-for-parade/?msclkid=eb30fca1d07e11ec9bd3c298259fa432.

[75] *Touched by An Angel*, Season 5—Episode #9, "Psalm 151," air date 11/15/1998, CBS, writers John Masius & Martha Williamson, dir. Sandor Stern (Pasadena, CA: MoonWater Productions).

[76] "Testify to Love," *A Maze of Grace*, Avalon, released 1997, track #1, written by Ralph Van Manen, Henk Pool, Paul Field, & Robert Riekirk, Sparrow Records—a division of Universal Music Group, New York, NY.; *Touched by an Angel*, episode #9, "Psalm 151," time stamp 40:46-44:23; "Testify to Love," *Love Can Build a Bridge—Song of Faith, Hope, & Love*, Cracker Barrel edition (Nashville, TN: Curb Records).

THIRTY-TWO

[77] Glenn Frontin, *A River Calling* (127 E. Trade Center Terrace, Mustang, OK 73064: Tate Publishing and Enterprises, LC, 2007), p. 29. Used with permission.

[78] Isaiah 53:4a (KJV).

THIRTY-THREE

[79] Isaiah 40:31a (Geneva 1599).

[80] *Secondhand Lions*, directed and written by Tim McCanlies, released 9/19/2003, produced by David Kirschner, Corey Sienega, & Scott Ross.

[81] Camp Barnabas, established 1994 (P.O. Box 3200, Springfield, MO 65806-3200).

THIRTY-FOUR

[82] Lori Wagner Knisely, "Happy birthday?" *Peace By Piece* (blog), 12/22/2021, https://peacebypiece147491366.wordpress.com. Used with permission.

[83] Lisa Wool-Rim Sjoblom, *Palimpsest—Documents from a Korean Adoption* (175 Varick Street—Suite #9, New York, NY 10014: Drawn & Quarterly, a client pub. of Farrar, Straus, and Giroux, 2019), p. 44.

[84] Sara Dorow—edited by, *I Wish for You a Beautiful Life—Letters from the Korean Birth Mothers of Ae Ran Won to Their Children* (1368 Michelle Drive, St. Paul, MN 55123-1459: Yeong & Yeong Book Company, 1999).

[85] Lorraine Murray, "Why Are So Many Koreans Named Kim?" *Britannica.com*, http://www.britannica.com/story/why-are-so-many-koreans-named-kim.

[86] Wikipedia, "International adoption of South Korean children," https://en.wikipedia.org/wiki/International_adoption_of_South_Korean_children?msclkid=67148c96d14211ec915afa99deea4c93.

[87] Lisa Wool-Rim Sjoblom, *Palimpsest—Documents from a Korean Adoption*, p. unnumbered front of book.

THIRTY-FIVE

[88] Joni Eareckson Tada, *A Step Further* (Grand Rapids MI 49506, Zondervan Publishing House, 1980), p. 184.

[89] "The Robert Germain Thomas Story"—*Torchlighters* DVD, Episode #14 (produced by Voice of the Martyrs & Christian History Institute, Gateway Films—Vision Video, P.O. Box 540, Worchester PA 19490, 3/12/2015).

[90] Psalm 27:10 (Geneva 1599).

[91] Wikipedia, https://en.m.wikipedia, org/wiki/Brocken spectre.

Photo Credits

Min Soo as a Toddler (cover photo)—Choi, Jung Hee (gifted to Kim, Min Soo)

Omma & Min Soo—SWS, South Korea (gifted to Kim, Min Soo)

Min Soo Arriving in New York State—A.S. Hampshire

Min Praying (cover photo)—Carolyn Burns

Adoption Day—Judge David Klim's Court Clerk

Naturalization Ceremony—Carolyn Burns

Min's Dedication to the Lord—Laurie Ogden

Dad, Mom, & Min—S.G. Hampshire

Special Christmas Parade for Min—Karen Corbett

All Other Photos—Brian or Sarah Hampshire

APPENDIX

Curious Readers Want to Know: Q & A

Q) Is the story's timing accurate?

A) *Pretty much so! Min confuses hours, days, weeks, months, years—yesterday, today, tomorrow—before and after, so we corrected timing. Otherwise, readers might need a time machine to figure it all out.*

Q) Why don't we mention names of places we lived?

A) *Sometimes Min confused our locations' whens and wheres, so we stuck with regions instead. That, or we're in the witness protection pro...uh oh!*

Q) Do Min's brothers' wives have names?

A) *Of course, but Min often attributes the wrong wife to the wrong brother. Scandalous! To keep his story "more appropriate," they are "wife, wife," and "wife."*

Q) Did your pets have very long lives?

A) *From their mention in 1996 till they "vanish—but not like in thin air" we actually owned more than one dog and cat. It was hard for Min to differentiate, so they became "the dog" and "the cat." Simple!*

Q) Did you notice the chapter number where Min shares about 9/11/2001?

A) *Min insisted 9/11 be in Chapter 11. When an edit pushed it into Chapter 12, he cried, "You're changing history!" His fans protested on his behalf, so his scribe "put 9/11 back where it belongs."*

Q) Does Min still enjoy certain foods?

A) *Some things never change. Every morning, he wants to know the meal plans for that day. And rice is still his favorite!*

Q) How are Min's stuffed animals doing?

A) *Pretty well. They're divided by species on different shelves, facing forward, looking at Min with two eyes. Min reports one recently blinked.*

Q) Has Min achieved his Guinness World record pencil goal?

A) *Last count = more than 1,000. The current record holder owns "gob loads" more.*

Q) Does Min still have his little cars?

A) *Most of them. He shared some with a few other little boys. He treasures these as well as his little green bag and small backpack that came with him from South Korea in May 1993.*

The End ... *of these questions but not Min's!*

www.ingramcontent.com/pod-product-compliance
Lightning Source LLC
Chambersburg PA
CBHW071150130626
46553CB00004B/1601